Teaching GCSE English

Jim Bennett

HODDER AND STOUGHTON
LONDON SYDNEY AUCKLAND TORONTO

ISBN 0 340 40765 4

First published 1987

Typeset by Tradespools Ltd., Frome, Somerset
Printed and bound in Great Britain for
Hodder and Stoughton Educational,
a division of Hodder and Stoughton Ltd,
Mill Road, Dunton Green, Sevenoaks, Kent,
by The Eastern Press Ltd, Reading and London

Contents

Acknowledgments

Sincere thanks are due to: Stephen Clarke of the Leeds University School of Education for his simulation game 'Fourth Form Transfer'; Paula Johnson for her GCSE Mode 3 coursework unit on *A Kestrel for a Knave*; Jean Rose and her English classes for their brainstorming work represented in the photographs; James Woods for his essay on a piece of machinery and to the English Department at Roundhay School, Leeds, for their staunch support in the inauguration of three GCSE courses. I am also particularly indebted to Richard Knowles, manager of H. & A. John (Booksellers) Ltd, for his assistance in producing the manuscript.

The author and publishers also wish to thank the following for permission to use material in this book:
The Controller, Her Majesty's Stationery Office for the extract on p.9 from *GCSE The National Criteria – English*, and the Northern Examining Association for the specimen question which appears in the Appendix. The cartoons are by Mike Mosedale. The photographs are by George Thompson.

Introduction

In essence, GCSE is what we want, and, in terms of English, what most of us have been working towards for some time. The election to pursue coursework and to have maximum individual control over how our students are examined has been the predominating influence over approaches to the subject in the last decade at least. There will be some diehards who will regret the passing of the single final examination, but most will recognise that the prevailing trend is far more in keeping with the movement towards formative rather than summative assessment and the commonsense desire to let young people have control over their learning and the power to negotiate upon the basis of their own strengths. Although profiling has yet to be rationalised into a viable system acceptable to employers, parents, children and teachers alike, it is inevitable that the positive elements of assessing students in this way will lead to its foundation as an integral part of English education, whatever the subject. And English lends itself so well to in-course assessment!

Probably the overriding impression of the Phase Two training of teachers nationwide has been, predictably, that there is no body of knowledge to pass on. It is the concern of this book to reassure the many staff who feel that there isn't much to go on, that in fact the best of good practice in GCSE terms is already happening. Now is the opportunity for teachers to dictate to the exam boards the terms of assessment, and not the other way round. There is no better assessor of students' capacity and potential than the class teacher, and that is the strength that must be affirmed and reaffirmed in the early stages of GCSE.

It is worth emphasising that what we are about is the development of language competence and not merely assessment. The idea of a two-year course in which every element must be viewed in terms of assessment is anathema to most teachers. Coursework must not become what it can easily be for teachers who need the security of rigid examination criteria – a mere scalp-hunting exercise to meet a predetermined total of 'units' or assignments. Some will baulk at the idea of what GCSE is truly about: classes of children doing different things and moving in different directions, very frequently without direct 'control' by the teacher. On the other hand, that is not to suggest that GCSE advocates a free-for-all – anything but. Some overall course structure must exist in the minds of both teacher and department if our students are really going to develop their language skills. This is not a checklist approach, but a sense of purpose which establishes what a department values most in the plethora of possible teaching strategies.

Bullock defined reading, writing, listening and talking as the fundamental elements of language. GCSE now gives us the opportunity to plan integrated courses with materials and resources appropriate to our students' needs, not to infringe upon the individual freedoms of a single class teacher, but to support those teachers with a sense of security that they are doing the right thing, whilst allowing them to operate with shared resources and their own ideas. This book will advocate, therefore, departmental planning of a kind which good departments have always known and accepted as normality. Rather than fixed assignments which everybody shares, the structure should be in the shape of the assignments, rather than in their content, and should ideally be supported by an agreed assignment profile which can record the observations of teacher and pupil, even to the recording of negotiation which takes place.

Hands up in horror! (Weren't they during Phase Two?) Where do we get the time? Hopefully this book will suggest rather than prescribe an overall scheme of things which is more in keeping with the 1990s than the 1970s, in a world which will no longer reward students merely because they can parade a list of examination scalps, but which will require of them a flexibility and a self-confidence to cope with shifting employment, unemployment and periods of adult retraining. Their linguistic competence will be measured in ways that might make us ashamed of some of the comprehension tests we know we have given!

1 The National Criteria for English

INTEGRATION

▼ *Fig. 1*

Assessment Objectives

The Assessment Objectives in a syllabus with the title English must provide opportunities for candidates to demonstrate their ability to:

1. understand and convey information;
2. understand, order and present facts, ideas and opinions;
3. evaluate information in reading material and in other media, and select what is relevant to specific purposes;
4. articulate experience and express what is felt and what is imagined;
5. recognise implicit meaning and attitudes;
6. show a sense of audience and an awareness of style in both formal and informal situations;
7. exercise control of appropriate grammatical structures, conventions of paragraphing, sentence structure, punctuation and spelling in their writing;
8. communicate effectively and appropriately in spoken English.

Probably the most potentially rewarding aspect of the *National Criteria* for English is the emphasis on the 'interrelated and interdependent' (para. 2.2) nature of the skills outlined in the eight Assessment Objectives (Fig. 1). This is what many teachers have accepted as fundamental to their teaching since even before the advent of coursework.

The eight Assessment Objectives are sufficiently broad-ranging to embrace the best of existing practice and to provide opportunities for a widening perspective. The main aim in meeting the Assessment Objectives ought to be the creation of work schemes designed on a foundation of real experience, rather than fabricated exercises. If students can appreciate that their efforts have real application to a real context, they will not only be successfully motivated, but will also acquire useful practical language skills. Since we want our students to speak well, listen effectively, read with understanding and write incisively, the stimulus material that we use will have to be chosen sensitively enough to cater for extremes of ability as well as for its power to invigorate students' language. Although the logistical implications of undertaking such well-conceived realistic situations as the visit paid by Carol Jones and her students to a local art gallery (BBC/OU GCSE Inset Video–Oral English) might well be an unattainable ideal for heavily burdened staff, we should acknowledge favourably the spirit of this attempt to place students in circumstances that will make them not only committed and interested but also aware that their learning need not be compartmentalised into textbook exercises governed by the strictures of examinations.

Language and Literature

Integration, then, is a key concept of GCSE. It is a pity that the authors of the *National Criteria* for English could not see the inherent absurdity of their first paragraph, in which we learn that 'English is to be regarded as a single unified course' which 'may also lead to a separate assessment in English Literature'. Many departments will have long accepted that language and literature are inseparable elements of the 'subject' English. The majority of teachers of English recognise literature as one of the most potent stimuli for language development, and current language coursework submissions reflect the powerful influence of works of literature upon thematic topics and on generating discussion of important issues for writing. Two separate assessments, dependent on insular sets of coursework with their attendant moderation/standardisation procedures, no doubt inspire great concern over time availability in the fourth and fifth years, and teachers in schools with large entries will surely find that only the most rational and streamlined approach to coursework assessment will allow them to retain their sanity! We have surely missed a wonderful opportunity for true integration of language and literature which would rationalise teaching and assessment alike into a more manageable entity.

However, the presence of compulsory reading of both literary and non-literary texts in the language scheme is a step in the right direction, and even those students who do not undertake the study of literature as a separate subject will enjoy the benefits of a literature-based course.

Ideally, therefore, our response to GCSE will be to devise units of work which encourage students to engage in activities that will, for example, send them away from the classroom to seek information by reading, by asking people other than teachers, by writing letters, reports and articles to further their research, as well as to respond to their findings, and to listen to each other's experiences in the classroom of the world outside.

The separate assessment of oral English will be dealt with in a later chapter, but as with the separate literature course we might be permitted to raise a wry eyebrow at the consistency of the proposed ideal of an integrated course which has an isolated oral component. That this is so suggests an underlying reactionary view that what employers, parents and higher education establishments are really interested in is what students can do on paper. Whilst this may be an heretical interpretation, we can at least derive some comfort from the fact that those students with a competence in spoken English will be rewarded for it, when, under the old examination system, little account was taken of it. Our schemes of work must now enhance the development of classroom language and give it a status which has been recognised for a long time, but not, perhaps, encouraged as much as it should have been, because of the written assessment bias of the examinations of the past.

FAIRNESS

Another key concept which in fact is limited to a minor paragraph in the 'Aims of the National Criteria' and in the content of the Literature course is the idea of fairness. The reference in para. 1.3 of the English *Criteria* implies an acceptance of the need to avoid cultural bias, though sexual fairness is not mentioned. Perhaps we should adopt the freedoms of a broader interpretation of this paragraph and underline the significance of true concern for sexual and cultural equalities in the work of our schools; English, as no other subject, has the power to influence the entrenched attitudes of our society, and hope for the future well-being of this country will depend on the degree to which we can show our students, or encourage them to learn for themselves, that race and sex demand acceptance and respect.

APPROPRIATENESS

A third major concept besides integration and fairness is the idea of 'fitness for purpose'. The *General Criteria* prescribe that 'all examination components and assessment procedures should reflect and be appropriate to the nature of the subject, its educational aims and its assessment objectives' (para. 19(e)). In English, our concern will be to develop coursework that is not only in keeping with the stated assessment objectives, but is also appropriate to the needs of students in the testing circumstances of the world beyond school. 'Fitness for purpose' can also be interpreted more widely in its relationship with choice of materials and differentiation. GCSE must ensure 'that candidates across the ability range are given opportunities to demonstrate their knowledge, abilities and achievements' (i.e. to 'demonstrate what they know, understand and can do'). If this is so, all GCSE courses must now apply the principles of differentiation. Simply explained, differentiation provides the means by which all candidates, of whatever ability, may find work accessible and rewarding. In other words, it is the 'assessment of positive achievement'. Rather than penalising students for what they cannot do, we are rewarding them for what they can do, according to clearly defined criteria at every level of the examination/assessment from grade A to grade G in written, and from grade 1 to grade 5 in spoken English.

DIFFERENTIATION

The SEC/OU GCSE *Guide for English* helpfully outlines the nature of differentiation as it is to be interpreted with regard to English. Whilst we can acknowledge the value and significance of ensuring that all students are provided with opportunities for adequately displaying their potential, we must not forget that the subject has always been fertile in its flexibility, and few of us would wish to be pinned down to a limited series of assignments set because they have proven qualities of differentiation. This is a very subjective area on which no two teachers will think alike, and on which examination boards will find it virtually impossible to investigate to what extent differentiation has been used. The logical conclusion is that, as with all coursework in the past, teachers are primarily in control of the manner in which schemes of work are prepared and tackled, and are to be *trusted* to know what is best for themselves and their pupils. To those of us who have known mixed-ability teaching organised either as school policy or because individual classes have been established upon grounds other than English, with resulting breadth of ability range, 'differentiation' minus its title has been the feature of a sensitive awareness that students need differing degrees of guidance and support, different amounts of stimulus and a varied measure of encouragement to enable them to fulfil their potential.

We can all provide examples of questions, papers and sections which have proven differentiation implicit in the language used to set them in their ascending scale of difficulty and in the mark schemes developed to assess them, but it would have to be the most arrogant of teachers who could claim to have got it right, however much time and effort were to be expended in doing it; at best, the mark schemes which indicate 'the expected positive qualities to be revealed by candidates of differing abilities' in dealing, for example, with differentiation by outcome (when students of all abilities respond to a common task and show their respective merits in the resulting work done) would be merely a tentative estimation. We surely cannot be expected to provide a mark scheme for every topic, especially when in the true spirit of GCSE we should be offering our students a broad range of options within any one topic and, indeed, encouraging students to pursue their own inclinations.

In the case of strategies for differentiation other than by outcome, extensive pre-testing of stepped questions and stepped papers would be logistically impossible except for such common assessment occasions as mock examinations.

This is not to say, therefore, that the principles of differentiation are absurd or impossible to achieve; it is to suggest that in the presentation of tasks to our students we employ automatically a process of differentiation of which, in practice, even the teacher involved would not necessarily be aware. The subject has no body of knowledge which could prove inaccessible to students. Whilst works of fiction commonly in use in schools and colleges vary considerably in grammatical and structural complexity, few teachers would think of getting students to undertake final assessment work arising from the reading of such texts without the most elaborate and exhaustive preparatory discussion and consideration of issues central to the task. Furthermore, having given students choice, teachers will inevitably direct immediate guidance to those of weaker ability to prevent their selection of topics beyond their capacity. Coursework at least ensures that we can avail ourselves of this less obvious kind of differentiation.

To highlight the problems facing teachers in achieving adequate differentiation, it is worth considering one assessment element over which we have the greatest opportunity for control over the demands made upon students: comprehension tests set either as external examination assessment or exercises done as part of coursework. The specimen examination paper provided by the Northern Examining Association (see the Appendix) illustrates how problematical it is to achieve differentiation, even in a context as strictly controlled as a formal comprehension. It is only fair to the board to quote its comment on the paper: 'the questions have not been subjected to the rigorous review which would take place with the draft question papers before use in an examination'.

The passage is an enjoyable one, which goes down well with classes when it is read aloud. Students enjoy the humour at Jude's expense and find the subject matter interesting. However, though 'the length of passages used need not in itself be a problem for candidates' (GCSE English *Guide*, p. 14), the length of this specimen comprehension would under examination conditions undoubtedly be disadvantageous to the weakest candidates, who often do not have the ability to retain content, though they may understand it. Even though the earlier questions employ inclusive line references to limit the range of answers, the text areas for consideration are still extensive (about forty lines). If we wish to ensure a positive experience for all candidates, there is a strong case for using stepped questions to enable the weaker students to find a way in. The examiners surely should also instil a sense of purpose in the questions, so that candidates are led towards the demonstration of an overall understanding of the central issue, namely the growth of adolescent awareness and its impact upon the mind of the central character. As it is, the questions are neither stepped nor represent a coherent interpretation. The apparent logic is merely chronological, which, to be fair, is a feature of most conventional comprehensions and can be supportive to the less able. Yet the first three questions represent what has been typical of this kind of paper: they have been chosen because there is a handy range of explicit information for literal comprehension, not for any deliberate attempt to illustrate the crucial issues. Questions 1 and 3 ('Describe Jude's home and family' and 'Describe the kind of neighbourhood where Jude lives') both expect literal comprehension. Why have both? A candidate who can manage one ought to be able to deal with the other! Why separate them by a question which makes use of explicit details, but requires some harder inferential interpretation? The mark scheme, incidentally, is haphazard, since we might have expected questions 1 and 3 to have equal weightings!

These early questions ignore the interesting and very relevant details about Jude's interpretation of his brother's attitude and of his sister's behaviour. The opening passage has plenty of factual information that could illustrate how well candidates understand that Jude is still a child, with a naive way of thinking and little concern for adult preoccupations of cleanliness and modesty. How much better it would have been to focus on these preliminaries to the later central scene.

A further criticism might be made of the third question which, apart from being of minor significance, could prove difficult for candidates without experience of urban terraced housing. It is not altogether clear whether comments on both the houses/streets and the people are expected, nor how many points should be made; eight or ten are possible – does this mean that candidates are penalised because they don't say enough, even if they understand fully? Question 4 expects not only selection skills, but also quite sophisticated critical interpretation of authorial method that even the best candidates would find difficulty in expressing succinctly and pertinently. In most cases, the likely response to a question of this nature would be a list of words correctly chosen, but inadequate commentary; students may *know* that these words indicate that the game meant a lot to the children, but find it difficult to say *how* they know. As in previous questions, we could ask why such a question has been asked anyway; presumably there is some intention to illustrate the contrast between the 'before' and 'after' feelings of Jude and Jane, but the question does not imply it very well.

Line references cease with question 5; the whole of the latter part of the passage from 105 onwards might be considered fruitful material for abstracting relevant details, but there is no indication of how the five marks allocated will be apportioned to the three defined areas of Jude's behaviour, thoughts and feelings.

The evaluation question (no. 6) is rightly placed towards the end of the exercise, considering its inherent difficulty in terms of the use of selected material from the whole passage, as well as considerable inferential expertise. This too, however, could have focused on all the older members of the family, since the degrees of their failure to appreciate Jude's needs would provide a sound contrast to the earlier directed interest in Jude's subjective view of his experiences.

The final question is so placed because of its much more challenging demands for abstract ideas, symbols or figurative representations of the key issue of the passage, as well as for the identification of contrast between Jude/Jane and the other children. It is a good question and would be accessible to more candidates if the previous sequence of questions were better designed. Candidates should, according to the expectation of differentiation techniques, be able to experience an ongoing process of discovery that would culminate in the most subtle interpretations. Differentiation in this paper is insufficient to do that effectively.

The 'rigorous review' mentioned by the NEA hopefully would have considered shorter and more specific initial questions, revised the order and selection of areas for consideration and given more indication of the ways in which the marks are to be allocated. Hopefully too, the mark schemes would have been flexible enough to allow for any reasonable interpretations, bearing in mind the differences in perception between adult examiners and children, not to mention the broad ability range and diverse social and cultural backgrounds of the candidates.

A survey of this paper reveals just how difficult it is to differentiate with a consistent degree of success. Even papers based upon open-ended questions with high mark allocations can seriously hamper the comprehension performance of the most able candidates, not because they fail to understand, but because the degree of their understanding adversely influences their apportioning of time. The LEAG specimen paper can cause candidates to suffer in just this way by providing heavy mark weightings to each question, and by not indicating the expected length and depth of response. A trial of this paper illustrated clearly that, rather than discriminating between candidates, the paper succeeded in narrowing considerably the range of final scores. The fact that examination comprehensions are inadequate means of assessment has been one of the reasons why many departments have opted for a syllabus without an external examination component. Certainly, to test thoroughly the wide range of comprehension skills we must look beyond the one- to two-hour comprehension paper.

DEMONSTRATING OVERALL CAPABILITY

After differentiation, fairness and integration, the *National Criteria* document emphasises the need for assessment according to 'some notion of overall linguistic capability' (para. 6.2). An awareness of the inherent problems of compensating for the different levels of a candidate's performance on the various elements of the subject seems crucial to final grading. If the grade awarded will depend in practice upon the 'extent to which the candidate has met the assessment objectives overall', our preparation of coursework ought to be sufficiently attuned to those objectives to ensure that candidates have had the opportunity to demonstrate the various skills clearly enough for us to allow for the fairest overall interpretation of their worth. Although the intention of GCSE is that the objectives should not be assessed in isolation, nor 'that any one should either dominate or play an insignificant part in the assessment', teachers will find it incumbent upon them to provide reasonable evidence of the range of objectives within a candidate's final submission. This fact will determine not only an individual teacher's design for an assignment, but also the strategies adopted by whole departments. The practical interpretation of this in terms of time and departmental management will be discussed later.

The conclusion to be drawn from the whole of the *National Criteria* document is that GCSE will enhance the quality of teaching because of its fundamental acceptance of the need for variety within structure, for a closely-woven fabric of reading, writing, speaking and listening, and for a sensitive response to the needs of all pupils as individuals.

2 Choice of Syllabus

STRENGTHS AND LIMITATIONS

Theoretically, we are to be permitted to choose whichever syllabus we wish. Already the logistical difficulties of this freedom of choice have become apparent in terms of agreement trials and standardisation meetings, when travelling distance means both time and money. Nevertheless, local groups can be formed through authority liaison to remove the necessity for individual centres of travelling vast distances and of having to consider overnight accommodation. Arguably, centres should not have to foot the bill even if local groups cannot be organised.

In the end, the prime consideration must be the choice of syllabus which is most suited to our students and ourselves, and which allows our candidates to capitalise on their particular strengths. In addition, English departments must consider how literature is to be 'taught'. Depending on allocation of time and staffing, the presence of two English subjects in the curriculum can influence the selection of syllabus; whilst they are mutually supportive, the two courses do present a substantial coursework commitment, with the associated burden of additional external meetings as well as more administration. Obviously, English departments in some centres will be at a disadvantage in terms of staffing and lesson allocation, and need to influence curriculum planners to achieve something like equality between centres. Few other subjects have anything like the marking (and soul-searching!) task faced by the English teacher; English departments in some large centres will, however well-organised they are in their handling of GCSE, find individual colleagues dealing with as many as four sets of literature and language coursework in the fifth year, perhaps with a time allocation little better than for a single subject. The local authority advisory divisions might perhaps be called upon in cases of extreme necessity to add weight to our case for a sensible slice of the curriculum cake!

Assessment

At this moment (late 1986), departments have made their initial selection of syllabus for 1988; their subsequent policy will of course be related to the success of this first choice, which, in the nature of all things new, might not be the fairest test of the merits of an examination assessment course. Departments with no experience in coursework will inevitably find these first two years traumatic for their strangeness and for their entirely different administrative responsibility. The compulsory oral component will in itself present seemingly insurmountable problems in both testing and recording achievement. Do we elect to pursue the syllabus with 100 per cent coursework if we have found the coursework examination to be extremely demanding? If we have decided upon 100 per cent coursework, how do we deal with the more troublesome of our students between the completion of the coursework files and the departure date for the examinations? Even though we have already been engaged upon 16+ courses with 100 per cent coursework, and find such courses entirely appropriate, do we still feel comfortable about the amount of continuous assessment work in both literature and language? Many of us value the absolute control that complete coursework allows us; many of us will be relieved to see the back of sterile regurgitative exercises that have accompanied O level literature examinations; yet the reality of our experience as teachers of English is often very different from the ideal. If we are to survive, smiling, with just a touch of private life left to us, are we going to be obliged to discount our ideals a little and, say, do one course with 100 per cent coursework and the other with part-examination? Are we seriously going to ditch literature examination/assessment courses altogether and, in the true spirit of GCSE, integrate our teaching along a single track? And if we do choose this single-course approach, are we going to be in conflict with parents and school management teams who really only value the number of examination results our students can acquire, rather than the overall quality of their education, and insist on English departments' production of two grades?

Post-16 Provision

Another unknown quantity for consideration in our forward thinking concerns the post-16 provision. While A level courses exist in their present form, are we really providing the most valuable foundation for the most academically inclined of our students? We must certainly take account of the needs of such candidates in a true perspective of 11–19 education; this minority must not, in our departmental management of GCSE, be prevented from being stretched to reach their potential.

All these questions, and no doubt many others of a similar kind, have already occurred to us; two further years' teaching towards GCSE may not have answered them satisfactorily. It will be vital for all teachers of English to recognise that their shared experiences can ultimately influence the shaping of GCSE in the future so that the best of it will be sustained.

Although the national criteria have standardised many of the syllabus approaches to assessment in English, there still remains a pleasing variety of possibilities for our appraisal. No doubt the examination groups will wish to avoid a proliferation of Mode 3 examinations in the future, though, as will become clear from this chapter, such internally developed courses are by no means a thing of the past.

Aural Assessment

Only one examination group (MEG) offers us the option of aural assessment; this is surprising, since the truly integrated courses envisaged by the Secretary of State would suggest the inclusion of some assessment of listening skills. Aural tests have been included in certain Mode 3 English and Communications examinations before, notable examples being those presented by a Bradford consortium and some Leeds schools to the Yorkshire and Humberside Regional Examinations Board. These were developed specifically to accommodate the needs of students from a variety of ethnic backgrounds with English as their second language. So useful have they been that they have proved invaluable to many English children who have suffered severe retardation in their own language development and have reached the school-leaving age without any hope of success in Mode 1 examinations. The MEG aural test will not present too many practical difficulties – the provision of a cassette tape by the board, appropriate play-back equipment and rooms with reasonable acoustics are all that is required. Centres with experience of the JMB Overseas Test in English are already aware that such tests can be easily conducted. Perhaps the other examination groups will in the future offer the option of a syllabus with an aural test.

Written Assessment

For the written assessments, all the examining groups have offered the choice of 100 per cent coursework assessment. Such assessment involves the centre in 'agreement trials', which, as those who have already had experience of them know, are a very fruitful and stimulating way of generating ideas for coursework as well as of achieving an expertise in assessing candidates' work. These trials also ensure that there is a regular forum for teachers to influence the board. In the case of the NEA, three separate trials are to be held, two externally and one within the centre. Teachers from the centre will be expected to serve as inter-school assessors on the 'review panel'. The SEG will operate a consortium marking 'workshop' arrangement requiring attendance by the teacher responsible for internal standardisation within each centre. The other boards, likewise, propose to train a representative from each centre for the standardisation of assessments as well as using exemplar material and consortia meetings.

CHOOSING A SYLLABUS

Like all choices, the selection of a syllabus appropriate to the needs of a centre will depend upon the fine reconciliation of conflicting elements. Whilst a 'better the devil you know' approach will probably have determined initial choices, under the pressure of severe time constraints, departments may well be prepared to sample courses offered by other boards, once the whole system has had a chance to settle. What are the criteria for our judgements?

Criteria for Choice

1 Do the administrative arrangements of an examining group overburden us? Clearly, the weight of administration will be of concern to many teachers, and when so much of the final year of the course will be lost to us as far as teaching and learning are concerned, we shall no doubt be conscious of the number of external meetings that take us from our classes, and of how early we shall need to call a halt to coursework to enable us to complete the rigorous scrutiny of folders of work and the secretarial tasks before submission. Dates, therefore, are important; the later the better. As for the administration, the simpler and more streamlined the methods of an examination group can be, the more likely are we to do our part of the procedure successfully.

2 How much coursework is required? The variation in the number of pieces required is slight (for the 100 per cent coursework syllabus, the SEG requires twelve pieces; the other groups ask for ten).

3 In the case of a syllabus with coursework and an examination, what percentage weighting is given to each component? Considering the commitment demanded by any coursework element, it might seem preferable to opt for a reasonably high percentage (all the boards except the MEG offer 50 per cent coursework in syllabuses of this kind).

4 What kind of examinations are on offer, and how well differentiated are they? At this stage, specimen papers offer a very uncertain guide as to the shape of things to come, but, as we have already seen, the difficulties of providing examinations which cater adequately for all abilities can be enough to recommend the pursuit of coursework alone.

5 Does the length of examination papers matter to our candidates? (Times of papers on offer vary from 1 hour 30 minutes to 2 hours 15 minutes.) In some syllabuses there is more than one paper.

6 How much freedom is given us in the selection of material for final assessment? Teachers will probably prefer to play to the strengths of their candidates if they can; thus the NEA's realistic awareness of the value of flexibility in terms of different categories of writing might be preferable to the very precise expectations of the SEG. Certainly the idea that students' writing does not have to fit rigid predetermined categories is a pleasing indication that at least one group has already foreseen the likely problems about deciding whether a piece of writing is of one kind or another. Even the 'simple' task of discriminating between fictional and factual writing has led to heated argument!

7 How much freedom is permitted in the assessment of oral English? Whilst we can accept the examiners' concern that pupils experience a true variety of oral contexts, we probably

would prefer not to be limited by such constraints, as identified by the SEG. (The chapter on oral English will further develop the discussion of this topic.)

8 Are we able to select a method of recording assessment in spoken English which suits our needs? Realistically, the hair-splitting fastidiousness of checklists might look very well on paper, but is extremely difficult to follow in practice.

9 Is none of the published syllabus combinations appropriate to our candidates? No doubt the examination groups will have hoped to have provided so comprehensive a range of different courses as to obviate the need for centres to submit Mode 3 syllabuses for consideration. Such is the variety of educational establishments, and so great the range of student ability, that some centres will wish to establish a Mode 3 course.

Considering the haphazard provision of syllabus booklets during the last six months, it is probable that departments will not have had the fairest conditions for making a truly objective appraisal of what is on offer. More questions than these will be raised during the next two years. Ultimate choices will have to depend upon experience!

Survey of Syllabuses

The outline (Figs 1–3) of the chief characteristics of the syllabuses on offer may be helpful in narrowing the choice. If there is indeed no Mode 1 course available that will accommodate a centre's particular needs, the creation of a Mode 3 scheme remains a possibility, though the examination groups are likely to be more rigorous than ever before in their scrutiny of such schemes; a centre's justification of a Mode 3 will therefore have to ensure that it is indeed breaking new ground.

CREATING A MODE 3 SYLLABUS

An obvious possibility is the construction of syllabus that will integrate language and literature into a 'single unified course'. Where a department finds itself under severe time constraints so that only sufficient lesson allocation for one course is available, there might well be the perfect opportunity for combining language and literature.

There has always been a dilemma over literature provision. Some centres have literature as an option; others have managed to cope with it within a total English lesson allocation of as low as five per week. Some centres have many candidates; some few. Considering these variables, those centres in the least advantageous position (with little time and great student demand) will see a Mode 3 as the obvious course of action. To give literature a reasonably high profile without overburdening teaching staff with marking and assessment work (especially those staff with more than one class in the final year), a Mode 3 can be the answer.

▼ *Fig. 1 Syllabus summary: LEAG/MEG/NEA/SEG Syllabus A*

LEAG	(No syllabus code) *Paper 1* Coursework 50% 5 units of 400–500 words range of kinds not prescribed	AND	*Either: Paper 2* Written paper (2¼ hours) 50% Two + passages/range of kinds Understanding and response *Or: Paper 3* Coursework 50% Understanding and response 5 units of 400–500 words (Response to a range of texts of various kinds)			AND	*Paper 4* Oral coursework 50% of total oral marks AND *Paper 5* Oral test 50% of total oral marks
MEG	SCHEME 1 *Paper 1* (aural) 50 mins 20% *Paper 2* (written) 1¾ hours 50% *Section A:* Directed writing – informative/factual stimulus (20%) *Section B:* Continuous writing – personal, descriptive, narrative. One piece 350–600 words (30%) *Coursework:* Four pieces: 30% 1 Personal/descriptive/narrative (min. 400 words) 1 Argumentative/informative 2 Response to literature/reading	OR	SCHEME 2 *Paper 1* (aural 50 mins 20% *Coursework* Eight pieces – 80% 2 Understanding 1 Personal/descriptive/narrative (min. 400 words) 1 Argumentative/informative 2 Response to literature/reading 2 Other	OR	SCHEME 3 *Coursework* 100% ten pieces 2 Understanding from listening and reading 1 Personal/descriptive/narrative (min. 400 words) 1 Argumentative/informative 2 Response to literature/reading 4 Other	AND	*Oral* Compulsory five different speech activities.
NEA	*One paper only:* *Written* (2 hours) 50% *Section A:* Questions on literary passage(s) *Section B:* Continuous writing related to passage in section A	AND	*Coursework* 50% 1 Understanding non-literary material 2 Factual/argumentative (closed) 2 Narrative/imaginative/personal (open)			AND	*Oral* A wide variety of tasks (no prescription) engaging listening and speaking.
SEG	*Paper 1:* *Written* (1½ hours) 25% *Section A:* Understanding/appreciation (max. 6 questions) *Section B:* Directed writing (1 question) [Literary passage(s)]	AND	*Paper 2:* *Written* (1½ hours) 25% Directed writing from factual/graphical/statistical stimulus (max. 5 questions)	AND	*Paper 3:* *Coursework* 50% 6 Pieces (total 2,500 words): 2 Response to literature 1 Descriptive 1 Narrative 1 Creative	AND	*Oral* Three contexts: Compulsory pair work, group work, individual work.

LEAG	No syllabus B.						
MEG	SCHEME 1 *Paper 1* (written) 2 hours 35% Argumentative/informative From diagrammatic/graphic stimulus. *Paper 2* (written) 2 hours 35% Personal/expressive From prose, poetry or drama stimulus. *Coursework:* Four pieces 30% 1 Response to reading (min. 400 words) 3 Other.	OR	SCHEME 2 *Coursework* 100% ten pieces 2 Understanding from reading 1 Personal/descriptive/narrative (min 400 words) 1 Argumentative/informative 2 Response to reading 4 Other	AND	*Oral* Compulsory five different speech activities.		
NEA	COURSEWORK 100% 10 pieces: Range of kinds of writing not prescribed (except 1 piece understanding of and close response to literature)	AND	ORAL A wide variety of tasks (no prescription) engaging listening and speaking.				
SEG	COURSEWORK 100% 12 pieces 2 Expressive/imaginative (min. 2 max. 5) 2 Discursive/argumentative (min. 2 max. 5) 2 Explanatory/instrumental (min. 2 max. 5) 4 of total based on reading of literature 2 of total based on non-literary material	AND	ORAL Three contents: Compulsory pair work, group work, individual work.				

▲ *Fig. 2 Syllabus summary: LEAG/MEG/NEA/SEG Syllabus B*

▼ *Fig. 3 Syllabus summary: LEAG/MEG/NEA/SEG Syllabus C*

LEAG	No syllabus C.						
MEG	No syllabus C.						
NEA	PAPER 1 2 hours 50% *Compulsory* Comprehension and response – writing for different purposes	AND	*Either: Coursework* 50% 5 pieces: 1 Response to reading 1 Narrative/imaginative/personal 1 Argumentative/opinion/reporting + 2 from above 3 types. *Or: Paper 2* written 50% (for external candidates) *Section A* Literary passage understanding/response *Section B* 1 Piece personal/imaginative continuous writing.	AND	*Oral* A wide variety of tasks (no prescription) engaging listening and speaking *But* Oral test for external candidates.		
SEG	PAPER 1 1¾ hours 40% *Section A:* Narrative: 1 story in response to theme. *Section B:* Argument: 1 piece expressing opinion. Stimulus materials given to students 15 days before exam.	AND	PAPER 2 2 hours 40% Understanding and response 2 + passages	AND	COURSEWORK 20% Thematic 2000 words max. 1 Single or up to 5 pieces including response to 1 whole work of literature.	AND	ORAL Compulsory pair work, group work, individual work.

Where else could a Mode 3 be helpful? There are schools and colleges, particularly in the inner cities, where the range of student ability is enormous. In spite of differentiation, there will be candidates who, because they are very retarded in English skills, will not really have the opportunities for fulfilling their potential by the pursuit of Mode 1 courses. Experience has shown that many pupils below the eightieth percentile have been entered successfully in the past for Mode 3 courses. No doubt this will be the case in the future.

The Mode 1 examination syllabus which has a combination of final examination and coursework may very well not be accessible to students of very low ability, simply because the mere length of passages to test understanding defeats them, or because the questions formulated (however carefully!) do not allow the candidate to grasp the nature of what is required. Such candidates (perhaps they are second-language learners) can within a secure context comprehend abstract concepts and draw inferences; it is therefore imperative that we tailor examinations to fulfil their needs. The incentive value of an end-of-course examination for very weak pupils has long been recognised; the very training in dealing logically and meticulously with examination techniques is in itself very valuable at this level.

Though 100 per cent coursework assessment might seem to be useful, there is often an unwritten implication (and often explicitly stated, too!) that coursework should be of substantial length, which is again beyond the capabilities of the least able. We have found their needs best served by the provision of courses with short-term aims and more easily accessible goals to build confidence, offering, as valid assessment material, exercises which do not fit the mould of an established Mode 1 course. There is no reason why such Mode 3 courses should not incorporate very demanding activities, such as some extended writing and texts of sufficient difficulty to offer challenge and interest. However, whilst Mode 1 courses might not accept such specific skills tests as sequencing, cloze tests and basic language work, these can very well be included in coursework assessment for a Mode 3. Perhaps more importantly, at this level, a Mode 3 will allow us to incorporate connected and coherent schemes of work that will weld coursework and final examination together.

The following 'unit' of work has been prepared for inclusion in a GCSE Mode 3 submission, as part of the coursework component (there is also an end-of-course examination) which consists of a range of units based upon language and literature topics. Though the novel chosen is less in vogue amongst teachers these days, it is still a firm hit with teenagers! It will be seen from the nature of the tasks set that the course is aimed at low-ability children who need much more support, through carefully structured questions and coherent overall organisation. The unit is as much a teaching as an assessment tool, for developing skimming, scanning, note-taking, drafting, etc., as well as for leading students to a reasonable grasp of the whole of the text. The range of choices is more limited than might be expected of a Mode 1 coursework assignment, since the weakest candidates benefit considerably from close guidance; it goes without saying that careful teacher–student consultation will accompany each section.

GCSE Mode 3 Literature Assignment on *A Kestrel for a Knave* by Barry Hines

I Understanding

Read the following extracts, then answer the questions in your own words and as clearly and fully as possible. Check that you have included all the ideas that you can think of before you move on to the next question.

It is very early in the morning. In a dark bedroom which has no curtains Billy Casper and his elder brother Jud are trying to sleep in a large double bed. The alarm clock goes off and Jud switches it off...

Billy: Jud?
Jud: What?
Billy: Tha'd better get up.
(*There is a moment of silence.*)
Billy: Alarm's gone off, tha knows.
Jud: Think I don't know? (*Nothing happens.*)
Billy: Jud?
Jud: What?
Billy: Tha'll be late.
Jud: O shut it.
Billy: Clock's not fast, tha' knows.
Jud: I said SHUT IT. (*He thumps Billy hard in the kidneys.*)
Billy: Gi' o'er! That hurts!
Jud: Well shut it, then.
Billy: I'll tell my mam on thi.
(*Jud thumps him again, then gets up.*)
Billy: Set t'alarm for me, Jud. For seven.
Jud: Set it thisen.
Billy: Go on, thar up.
(*Jud pulls the blankets off the bed.*)
Billy: You rotten sod, just because tha's to get up.
Jud: Another few weeks, lad, and tha'll be getting up wi' me.

1. What does this extract tell us about Jud and his behaviour towards Billy?
2. Why do you think Billy is so keen to get Jud out of bed?
3. Why does Jud say, 'Another few weeks, lad, an' tha'll be getting up wi' me.'? What does this tell us about Billy?

Having realised that Jud has taken his bike, Billy has to run to Mr Porter's newsagent's in order to do his paper round. Mr Porter is waiting for him impatiently.

Mr Porter: I thought you weren't coming.
Billy: Why, I'm not late, am I?
Mr Porter: Well, you're not early.
Billy: I nearly wa', though.
Mr Porter: What do you mean?

Billy: Late. Our Jud went to t'pit on my bike.
Mr Porter: What you going to do, then?
Billy: Walk it.
Mr Porter: Walk it! And how long do you think that's going to take you?
Billy: It'll not take me long.
Mr Porter: Some people like to read their papers t'day they come out, you know.
Billy: It's not my fault. I didn't ask him to take it, did I?
Mr Porter: No, and I didn't ask for any cheek from you! Do you hear? 'Cos there's a waiting list a mile long for your job, you know. Grand lads an' all, some of 'em. Lads from up Firs Hill and round there.

4. Describe Mr Porter's attitude towards Billy here. What kind of a person is he?
5. What does Mr Porter imply when he says 'Some folks like to read their papers t'day they come out'?
6. What do you imagine Firs Hill is like? How does it differ from the estate Billy lives on?

Billy returns home after his paper round. As he walks across the garden, a man comes out of the side of the house. When Billy goes in, he asks his mother about the man who has just left...

Billy: Who's that bloke?
Mrs Casper: That's Reg. You know Reg, don't you? (*She looks for a cigarette.*) Hell! I forgot to ask him for one. You haven't got a fag on you, have you, love?
Billy: Is that him you come home with last night?
Mrs Casper: There's some tea mashed if you want a cup, but I don't know if t'milk's come or not.
Billy: Was it?
Mrs Casper: Oh, stop pestering me! I'm late enough as it is. Do me a favour, love, and run up to t'shop for some fags.
Billy: They'll not be open yet.
Mrs Casper: You can go to t'back door. Mr Hardy'll not mind.
Billy: I can't, I'll be late.
Mrs Casper: Go on, love, and bring back a few things wi' you: a loaf and some butter, and a few eggs, summat like that.
Billy: Go yoursen.
Mrs Casper: I've not time. Just tell him to put it in t'book and I'll pay him at t'weekend.
Billy: He says you can't have owt else' til you've paid up.
Mrs Casper: He always says that. I'll give you a tanner if you go.
Billy: I don't want a tanner. I'm off now.
Mrs Casper: Billy, get up to that shop and do as you're telled.

7. What do these few lines tell us about Mrs Casper?
8. Why do you think Mrs Casper ignores Billy's questions about Reg and accuses him of 'pestering' her?
9. Why do you think Billy doesn't want to go to the shop for his mother?

After his English lesson Billy goes out into the playground for break. He stands on his own, but after a while Macdowall and some other boys come over to taunt him...

Macdowall: What's up, Casper, don't tha like company? They say thi mother does.

(*The boys begin to snigger and Billy turns his back on them.*)

Macdowall: I've heard tha's got more uncles than any kid in this city.

(*Billy turns to face them.*)

Billy: Shut thi mouth! Shut it, can't tha!

Macdowall: Come and make me.

Billy: Tha can only pick on little kids. Tha' daren't pick on anybody thi own size!

Macdowall: Who daren't?

Billy: Thee! Tha wouldn't say what tha's just said to our Jud. He'd murder thi.

Macdowall: I'm not frightened of him.

Billy: Tha would be if he wa' here.

Macdowall: Would I heck, he's nowt, your Jud.

Billy: Tha what! He's t'cock o' t'estate, that's all.

Macdowall: Who says? I bet I know somebody who can fight him.

Billy: Who? Thi father?

10. What do we learn about Macdowall from these lines?
11. Explain what Macdowall means when he says, 'They say thi mother does.'
12. What does Billy mean when he refers to Jud as 't'cock o' t'estate'?

After the fight with Macdowall breaks out, Billy is saved by Mr Farthing. Mr Farthing tells Macdowall off, then talks to Billy about how he is getting on . . .

Mr Farthing: Well, I shall have to go and blow the whistle, they've had five minutes extra already.

Billy: Good.

Mr Farthing: What do you mean?

Billy: It's games next, that means five minutes less.

Mr Farthing: Well, you'd better be off then and get cleaned up, or you're going to have no lesson left.

Billy: That'd be nice. It'll be an hour of purgatory on that field.

Mr Farthing: Billy.

Billy: What, sir?

Mr Farthing: This hawk of yours. I'd like to see it some time.

13. What do these lines tell us about Mr Farthing?
14. Explain what Billy means when he says that 'It'll be an hour o'purgatory on that field'. What is it that he dislikes about games?
15. Why do you think Mr Farthing takes an interest in Billy?

Billy ends up playing in goal for Mr Sugden's team, and as a result they lose. Mr Sugden has to get his revenge, so he makes Billy have a shower. He traps him and turns the water on cold.

Billy: Hey up, shift. Let me out, you rotten dogs.

Mr Sugden: Got a sweat on, Casper?

Billy: I'm frozen!

Mr Sugden: I thought you'd like to cool down after your exertions in goal.

Billy: Give over, sir, it's not right.

Others:	Can we let him out now, sir?
Mr Sugden:	No.
Others:	He'll get pneumonia.
Mr Sugden:	I don't care what he gets. He made me lose and he'll pay for it.

16. How is Mr Sugden different in his attitude towards Billy from Mr Farthing?
17. Why do you think the other lads eventually side with Billy?
18. What was Mr Sugden's favourite football team?

II Essay written as if you were Billy

Imagine that you are Billy. Write down your thoughts and feelings about your life. Use the diagram (Fig. 4) to help you, but feel free to add your own thoughts.

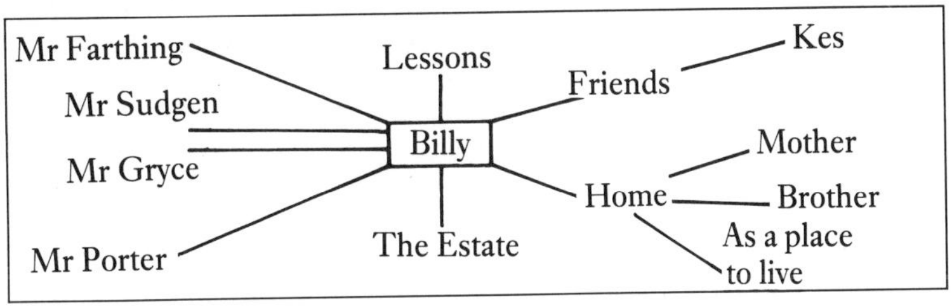

▲ *Fig. 4*

III Understanding/knowledge of the book

In order to answer the following questions you will have to know your way around the book – relying on your memory probably won't be good enough.

To find the answers to some of the questions you will have to flick through the book in order to find the right scenes; knowing the order in which scenes take place will help a great deal.

1. What jobs does Billy have to do before he goes to school in the morning?
2. Billy's breakfast consists of some rather unusual things. Explain what these things are and how Billy obtained them.
3. Why is it that Billy is unable to do his paper round on his bike?
4. What problem does Billy encounter when he tries to borrow a book from the library?
5. How does Billy get hold of the book he wants?
6. Billy and Jud do not get on well as brothers. State whether you agree with this statement and find some evidence to back up what you say.
7. Mr Gryce is a strict disciplinarian. Explain what you understand this to mean and show some evidence to prove it.
8. What nickname did the boys have for Mr Gryce?
9. Explain why it is that the messenger who goes to Mr Gryce's room is punished.
10. At several points in the book Billy falls asleep when he shouldn't. Give some reasons as to why Billy should be so tired.
11. Billy isn't very good at his school subjects, but when he finds a subject that he is interested in he is motivated. What proof can you find to support this statement?

12. What does Billy's 'tall story' tell us about Billy's feelings about his life? (Remember that what he writes is not true, it is what he wishes his life could be like.)
13. What were the names of the horses that Jud wanted to place a bet on?
14. What road was the fish and chip shop on, and what was its name?

IV Creative writing – a 'tall story'

Re-read what Mr Farthing says about writing a 'tall story'. Once you have understood what a 'tall story' is, write your own 'tall story' and make it as fantastic as possible.

V Language work – Billy's 'tall story'

Re-read Billy's 'tall story'. As you can see, it is riddled with mistakes in spelling and punctuation. Write Billy's story out again, but make sure that you have corrected all his mistakes – use the following list as a checklist to make sure that you are not repeating his mistakes.

Checklist: paragraphs
sentences (full stops, capital letters)
commas
apostrophes (to show possession and abbreviation)
question marks and exclamation marks
punctuation of speech
spelling

VI Newspaper report

Imagine that you are a journalist working for a local newspaper. You find out about the violent goings-on at the Casper household and decide to write an article about it. Your job is to write out the report and to present it as it would appear in a real newspaper.

1. Think of an eye-catching headline. Remember that headlines should be short and to the point; you want to attract people's attention but you don't want to give all the story away. For example, BIN BIRD HORROR or HAWK TRAGEDY would be better headlines than YOUNG BOY'S BROTHER KILLS FAMILY PET IN ARGUMENT OVER BETTING SLIP.

2. Write your report in rough. In order to make it realistic, you will have interviewed all the characters involved and also found out some background information about Billy from friends, family and school.

3. Write out your report just as it would appear in a newspaper. You will have to write out your headline in big bold letters and then write your report in columns underneath. To make it look even more convincing, you can divide your report up by using suitable sub-headings.

4. Cut out a photograph from an old newspaper, or draw a picture of one of the people involved in the story, and place it in an appropriate place in order to illustrate your story.

5. Make up some advertisements for local shops (the betting office, the newsagent's, the fish and chip shop, etc.) and put them above or below your report.

VII Oral work

Get into a group with other people that you work well with. The work that you will be doing will require you to act sensibly and to work in a co-operative fashion.

Your job is to write a play script based on the events of *A Kestrel for a Knave*. The play is to be broadcast on radio, and when you have finished writing it you will perform it as a group and tape it.

Points to bear in mind:

1. People cannot see what is happening on the radio; you will have to make it clear what people are thinking or feeling by introducing each scene and giving them lines which make it obvious.
2. When you write the script, think about sound effects that you want to include – how are you going to make them?
3. Don't attempt anything too complicated – it will be best to keep it as simple as possible.

Select three of the following scenes to perform:

a) The scene in the newsagent's before Billy does his paper round.
b) The scene in assembly and in Mr Gryce's room.
c) The fight scene and Mr Farthing's intervention.
d) Arriving late to Mr Sugden's lesson and in the showers afterwards.
e) Billy talking to Kes and training her.
f) The confrontation with Jud after the death of the bird.

VIII Cloze test on *Kes*

Put an omission mark (^) where you think a word has been missed out, then write the missing word in the space provided.

Barry Hines, the of *Kes* or *A Kestrel for a Knave*, 1 ______
was in the mining village of Hoyland Common, near 2 ______
Barnsley in 1939. His father had a as a miner in a 3 ______
local pit. Barry Hines Ecclesfield Grammar School and 4 ______
as he was very talented at football he was to play for 5 ______
the England Grammar Schools' Football Team.

After he school, he played football for the Barnsley 6 ______
'A' Team and also worked as apprentice mining surveyor 7 ______
and as an assistant in blacksmith's shop. He didn't do 8 ______
this for long, though, and later went on study Physical 9 ______
Education at Loughborough Training College.

Having finished his training, he to London and got a 10 ______
job as a teacher. He Physical Education at a large 11 ______
comprehensive school North London before deciding to 12 ______
move north again to Yorkshire. Now he a full-time 13 ______
novelist and scripts for television plays. 14 ______

Books like *Kes* and *Looks and Smiles* deal with the
problems facing young people who live in areas, where 15
jobs are hard to and people have to learn to live with 16
poverty. Probably because he from a mining community 17
himself, he also writes about the hardships faced by
those who work down the. 18

Kes was first published in 1966 and a best-seller.
It has since been made into a film and has been enjoyed 19
by old and people alike. 20

Assessment and content

Whatever our particular circumstances for the creation of a Mode 3 syllabus, we must address ourselves initially to the formulation of a convincing justification on educational grounds. As only a significant departure from an examination group's Mode 1 syllabuses can expect acceptance, the precise differences between the two will have to be made explicit. Since in English the assessment objectives will be largely common in the development of students' abilities to communicate effectively in the various language forms as well as to comprehend and interpret what they hear and read, it will be the nature of the scheme of assessment and the syllabus content which will embody the major differences. Obviously the proposal must comply with the subject national criteria. In addition, departments must expect to be able to determine clearly the educational aims of a Mode 3 syllabus and in what ways they can be achieved by the proposed scheme.

At this stage, the extent to which Mode 3 syllabuses will be in acceptance by the examination groups is uncertain. Centres may very well feel that a process of acclimatisation to GCSE is necessary before they make an objective assessment of the value of a Mode 3. However, the national criteria are clearly enough established to make the immediate inauguration of Mode 3 courses a worthwhile possibility; after all, there will always be candidates who benefit from the provision of Mode 3, and who will lose out if we delay.

3 Coursework and Examination

ADVANTAGES OF COURSEWORK ASSESSMENT

By now, most teachers of English will have some sense of the superiority of coursework assessment over final examination. The validity of a final examination is questionable in its limited sampling of candidates' written skills; the writing of one or two essays under strained circumstances cannot demonstrate the ability of a student to use language successfully in a wide range of contexts. The marking of examination scripts can be unreliable; it is certainly nowhere near as stringent or accurate as the work of teachers collaborating closely within a department and within a local consortium.

Coursework submissions, on the other hand, are accompanied by very detailed and explicit accounts of the circumstances under which candidates write, offering information as to purpose and audience, both of which are vital to any precise estimation of ability. This much fuller picture of the context for writing has an obvious advantage over the end-of-course examination. The degree of inter-staff communication and cooperation sharpens teaching methodology and assessment skills, enabling teachers to learn from the experiences of others as well as to influence others by their own ideas. Students are given much more favourable circumstances in which to write, against a background of wide-ranging stimuli, class discussion and personal consideration of a topic. Coursework therefore becomes a scheme for learning as well as assessment; its variety is its greatest merit.

This chapter will explore some possible strategies for coursework programmes as well as sample some of the end-of-course examinations on offer. The ultimate choice of syllabus will, as we have already seen, be determined by the particular needs and inclinations of individual departments.

COURSEWORK PROGRAMMES

It is probably as well to emphasise that material for assessment purposes should spring naturally from well-structured and stimulating coursework programmes. Since quality of candidate response should be more important than quantity, the length of submissions is of lesser significance. A good coursework file might demonstrate a candidate's written expertise in pieces of work of varying lengths; the inclusion of some substantial pieces could certainly illustrate a candidate's prowess in organisation and sequencing.

It is perhaps an easy, yet erroneous, assumption that the

culminating piece of a series of connected coursework tasks will be the most accomplished. It is surely an experience common to all teachers that students produce writing of admirable quality almost as a by-product of an assignment scheme; they seem not to respond anything like as well to the notion that at the end of an enjoyable and varied diet of reading, discussion, drawing, looking at pictures or playing with scissors and glue they will have to write an essay. An understandable reaction! We all know that the most exciting things in English lessons never quite fit the requirements of external examinations; for that reason, good coursework and practice ought to play down the assessment element, which can otherwise lead to a two-year course dreadful for its bludgeoning of students into meeting a minimum quota for an assessment folder.

The key to successful coursework is thus enjoyment; the more administratively nit-picking the external demands on teachers and students, the more prosaic and stereotyped the results will become. The sooner, therefore, that examiners and teachers reach an understanding that coursework submissions can be of any reasonable length or form, the more rapidly we will stimulate our students into fulfilling their potential and exercising their latent powers of ingenuity and influence. If there is to be bias in our work schemes for the final two years of compulsory education, let it be towards a minimum of final assessment, allowing for a maximum of creativity!

▲ *It is essential in GCSE to exploit group work.*

Coursework in English, far from being the excessive burden envisaged by those accustomed only to end-of-year examinations, is the most certain way to reconcile the many variables which influence our teaching. Now, more than ever before, when continuous assessment work will be common to all educational establishments, we have to get the balance between learning and assessment right, and that does not mean increasing the number of nervous breakdowns! Since English Language and English Literature will be taught simultaneously by many teachers under severe time limitations, the trade-off between these two 'subjects' will have to be fully exploited.

Review panel meetings, internal and external moderation and standardisation meetings, trial marking and the everyday business of looking at each other's work and sharing ideas will absorb quite a lot of time; but this is time well spent. It enhances departmental solidarity, and generates healthy and fertile discussion; it is worth every minute. However, this and the fact that coursework must be completed well in advance of the academic year does curtail the amount of time available for fourth- and fifth-year courses: hence departments will find that to adopt common practices and agreed maximum levels of assessment work will rationalise the coursework component into manageable proportions. Also, faced with more coursework across the curriculum, students could very well suffer the pressures of severe overloading by staff engrossed in their own subjects.

The implications for departmental management will be considered later. If we accept the premise that coursework is both desirable and possible, we can now look more closely at what can be achieved. Consider again the GCSE essentials: accessibility, variety and integration; next exploit the most effective teaching methods at our disposal – discussion, improvisation/role play, audio-visual stimuli, group work, good poems, plays and stories, research, theatre and other outside visits; add to these one of the most important ingredients of all, student participation in the planning, and you have the basis for good coursework.

All assignments will be and should be unique in range and variety, as well as in possible assessment products. As far as the written element is concerned, we shall be looking to the provision of both 'closed' and 'open' tasks, as specified in para. 5.4 of the *National Criteria* document. Coursework assignments can very easily present candidates with a choice of both closed and open writing opportunities, and it will be for us to determine, in consultation with students, what will be the ultimate selection for final assessment. Whilst it is not necessary to develop all coursework assignments with this balance of kinds of writing, it is nevertheless fairly easy to incorporate both and offers more scope for students to choose how best to exploit their skills.

While variety within assignments is obviously going to meet the criteria laid down by the board syllabuses, variety across the whole coursework submission is a perfectly attainable ideal. A possible range could include a literary-based assignment, a thematic, a vocational, a pragmatic, a fictional, a comprehension one, a media topic, a research exercise, a cultural, a historical one, and so on. An assignment could consist of a selection of titles to develop a particular style of writing (descriptive, narrative, factual, persuasive, interpretative and so on), or be an elaborate scheme of linked and interdependent tasks; such a scheme might have a greater or lesser degree of teacher 'control', depending on the extent to which teachers might wish to provide common activities to discriminate more finely between candidates. The following is an example of an assignment sequence with a vocational slant that intends to provide more opportunities for learning than for assessment.

GCSE Language Assignment: Getting a Job

Any part of this assignment can be submitted for assessment for the examination course. Once you have done what you feel able to do (having first discussed your intentions with your teacher), complete an assignment profile sheet which shows clearly what you have achieved and what you wish to be included in your final assessment.

Your teacher will use parts of the work for oral assessment and make a diary record of what you have achieved. You too should keep a separate diary of spoken English which an examiner might wish to see.

Stage one

A. Research

In groups of four to six, decide on all the places where you can find information about all aspects of preparation for finding, getting and doing a job. At the end of this session, each member of the group must take responsibility for finding out some useful information from one or more of the sources of information. (Possibilities might include writing letters, making visits in your own time, interviewing appropriate people, using careers library facilities, etc.)

Each member of the group should keep a diary record of all research work undertaken, including copies of letters, rough notes, dates and times of travel, etc.

B. Reporting back

A group should share its findings in enough detail for every member to make helpful notes.

Stage two

Individuals should now select any aspect of the range of information provided by STAGE ONE, and present a formal written article on this topic for class display. This can be as long as you wish.

Stage three

A. This will be whole-class consideration of a sample job application letter and c.v., and discussion of the most effective ways of presenting oneself by letter to a prospective employer.

B. In groups of four to six (not necessarily the same groups as in STAGE ONE), give yourselves roles as the key personnel of an imaginary firm that is seeking to employ a school leaver. Create a job and an appropriate advertisement so that other members of the class can apply for it. Everyone should keep a copy of the job advertisement and personal notes about the job.

C. On publication of the advertisements, all the members of a group must choose and apply for a job advertised by one of the other groups.

D. Study, in groups, the resulting letters and discuss the qualities and weaknesses of each.

Stage four: mock interviews

A. Whole class consideration of the nature and purpose of interviews.

B. Members of each group must organise a formal interview, with appropriate questions and factual information about the fictitious company.

C. Mock interview role play. (Hopefully every person in the class will be interviewed.)

D. Whole class analysis of the interviews – which candidates were successful/unsuccessful at interview? Why?

Stage five: continuous writing

This should be a composition of some length (600 words is a good target), in which paragraphing, grammar and punctuation will be assessed. Individuals may choose to write on an associated topic not suggested here. This is perfectly acceptable as long as you discuss it with your teacher first.

1. Write a story about someone's experiences in seeking a job.
2. Write a playscript about an interview.
3. Write two accounts of the same interview from the point of view of:
   a) the interviewer
   b) the interviewee.
4. Write an article for a school magazine in which you aim to help school leavers to 'find that job'.
5. Write a report for the school's careers officer on the work your class has done on this assignment.

Stage six: individual or group oral exercise

Every member of the class must participate in and make a diary record of one or more of the following:

1. Personal account to teacher of any aspect of the work done, with factual information and opinions or reflections.
2. Improvise a piece of role play with the title 'How *not* to conduct an interview'.
3. Present a helpful dramatised documentary to a group of fifth-formers on how to look for and gain a job.
4. Interview a careers teacher, careers officer, employer or employee and report back to the class with a full spoken report of the interview.

Overview

This assignment, aimed at late-fourth or early fifth-year students, is designed for use in a school with a strong and supportive careers department. The timescale for its completion would be very much at the discretion of the teacher, especially in Stage One, when the ability level and degree of motivation of candidates will determine how much time is needed. Certainly, it is a good idea to offer deadlines, since it is of value to students to appreciate the kinds of pressure which they will undoubtedly experience in their working lives. In any case, since GCSE will incorporate coursework into the whole school curriculum, it is only fair to give students as much leeway as possible in the organisation of their time.

A crucial factor in presenting an assignment sequence to a group is having the whole assignment prepared for preliminary discussion and overview. This way, students can perceive the intention and direction of the scheme, can be given a chance to suggest alterations, deletions or insertions, and can handle parts of the topic in any order, according to their inclinations. As it happens, this particular assignment does depend on a developing sequence, though other topics might well be subdivided into units of work which can be tackled in any order.

The bias of this assignment is very much towards spoken English, and does presuppose class familiarity with group work and role play. It is helpful to indicate to students what aspects of the assignment might be considered appropriate for assessment. Students can then elect to focus their attentions upon things which interest them most, and upon which they are therefore likely to perform to best advantage. The GCSE offers us a degree of flexibility that we should exploit to the full; however, for those not accustomed to teaching through coursework, it might be disconcerting to have whole classes engaged on very different activities.

The prime aim of this assignment is not assessment, but to give students a working knowledge of skills which they will have to use beyond school. Schools and colleges with active careers departments and careers officer interviews can capitalise upon a resource that in fact can save English teachers time and effort; for example, a whole-class visit to the careers room can involve students in active listening to an objective expert and can open doors to an incredible wealth of factual printed material that students can use in a variety of ways. Furthermore, English teachers will immediately see ways of enriching a base assignment, in this case perhaps by looking at literary sources such as Billy Casper's careers interview in *A Kestrel for a Knave*, or inviting outside speakers from employment, Jobcentres and the like. This assignment, then, could be common to all candidates in a centre in its bare essentials, but its ultimate assessment value will and should depend on the inclinations of both teachers and students. The idea of a bank of such printed resources (stored on a computer, of course, and printed out at the touch of a button!) does sound enticing, but perhaps is dangerous in its suggestion that such assignments are fixed and inflexible. We do, after all, get the most mileage out of topics used regularly and adjusted by departmental discussion, however casual.

Another effective way of developing coursework is to begin with drama. The exploration of a fictional situation or one based on a real news event can open the eyes of students to the objective understanding of and empathy with the characters involved. Local or provincial newspapers are always a rich source of suitably sensational material, which has the stimulus value of human interest in a familiar setting. The following assignment, based upon a typical local news event, makes use of lots of traditional methods used in English lessons and can be given whatever slant teachers and classes prefer.

GCSE Language Assignment: Newspaper Drama

YORKSHIRE GUNMAN HOLDS WIFE HOSTAGE

Shots – then police rush gunman and save wife

Armed police today rushed a gunman holding his screaming wife hostage in a Yorkshire street.

Shouts were heard and a muffled noise followed as police officers ran up Ninelands Lane, Huddersfield, towards the gunman, and the girl's cries could be heard as waiting officers pulled her to safety.

Seconds later, the hysterical wife, dressed in a white skirt and blue blouse, carrying a white shoulder bag, was led, shaking, to an ambulance by police.

Earlier armed police wearing bullet-proof vests had sealed off the area as 20-year-old Steven Seabrook held his wife hostage for 90 minutes, armed with a gun and a knife.

It is believed that Seabrook comes from Gomersal and is on the dole. Police had also sent for his parents. Initially Seabrook, who is believed to have at least two children by his wife, and possibly another two children by another woman, demanded money, and officers at the scene had an emergency 'whip-round'.

Superintendent Edwards, who rushed the gunman, was seen being patted on the back – his shirt apparently covered at the front with blood. It was not immediately clear whose blood this was or how the police officer's shirt came to be soaked in it.

The drama began at lunchtime when two shots rang out.

Police marksmen rushed to Ninelands Road, Huddersfield after two shots rang out. A screaming girl fell to the ground – but passers-by were forced away by a pistol-waving youth standing over her.

As police marksmen with high-calibre rifles moved in, the youth forced the girl hostage further up the street. The girl could be heard screaming as the gunman continued to shout at police.

A witness, Mr Anthony Bryce, of Lovejoy Lane, Featherstone, had been on business in Huddersfield and was returning to his car parked nearby. While walking through the nearby railway station, he heard the sound of two shots ring out. When he got to Ninelands Road, he saw a girl who was sobbing, lying on the pavement. Standing behind her, shouting, was a youth holding a pistol. An elderly man went towards the youth, but the youth pointed the gun at the man and the man retreated.

Mr Bryce then withdrew into a nearby flat and called the police.

A woman at Huddersfield County Court, on Ninelands Road, said staff there could see the incident from a window. 'We can see a man with a gun holding a girl hostage,' she said. 'We have been told not to go out of the Ninelands Road door,' the woman added.

There was speculation that the couple had just attended a hearing at Huddersfield County Court, where there had been divorce hearings during the morning.

Stage one: group work

From your reading of the newspaper article, brainstorm (using newsprint and felt-tipped pens) the possible reasons for the situation described, and produce ideas about the personalities and their circumstances. Then produce a map that you think could represent the situation as described, showing clearly the relative positions of the police, the gunman and his wife, and the named spectators. This map should be of the kind printed in newspapers or shown on television to help the public to visualise the scene.

As a whole class, compare the different interpretations. Individuals will be asked to represent their group's point of view.

Stage two: improvisation

Explore through role play the situation as experienced by the participants in the drama. Choose as many as you like from the following list:

a) 999 call from member of public to the police (2 characters).
b) Husband and wife argument/dialogue at any stage of the drama (2 characters).
c) Group of spectators at the County Court building (2–4 characters).
d) Elderly man and gunman dialogue (2 characters).
e) Team of police marksmen and police superintendent (4 characters) preparatory to the arrest.
f) Police spokesman/gunman dialogue (2 characters).
g) Newspaper reporter/eye witness dialogue (2 characters).
h) Policewoman/wife discussion of events (2 characters) at the police station.
i) Police/newspaper reporter discussion (2 characters).
j) Newspaper reporter and colleague in the pub that night (2 characters).
k) Television newsreader on local evening news (1 character).

Stage three

Class discussion of the ideas arising out of the improvisation.

Stage four

A. Choose one of the following:

1. Write a commentary on the way this news article is written, showing how the newspaper tries to attract the attention of potential readers.

2. Rewrite the incident as a police officer might present it in a report. This should describe fully the activities of the police, including precise geographical details, the behaviour of the gunman and his wife, the results of the incident, an assessment of the operation, and any conclusions that might influence subsequent similar events.

3. As a member of the public, opposed to the use of firearms by the police, write a letter to the newspaper in which this story was printed, giving your views. Then write another letter to the editor in reply to the first.

4. Write two accounts of this incident: (a) the statement made by the gunman and (b) the statement made by his wife.

5. As a reporter, cover a real event and write a newspaper report of it.

B. Choose one of the following:

1. Write a story connected with this incident which brings to life the whole situation and the characters of the people involved, from the end of the divorce hearings to the questioning of the gunman after his arrest.

2. Write a playscript of the court case which followed this incident.

3. Write a story about another sensational news event.

4. Choose a newspaper headline or a photograph taken from a newspaper and write a fictitious newspaper article to go with it, complete with newspaper heading.

5. Write a part of the gunman's autobiography as he might have written it in prison.

Stage five

Collect and read as many newspaper reports involving the police as you can.

Stage six

Invite your Community Constable or a prison officer to talk about his/her work.

Overview

As with the assignment sequence on 'Getting a Job', the range of choice offers openings to all abilities. Differentiation also implies the presentation of various activities appropriate not just to ability, but also to inclination and preference. The wider the choice, the more likelihood there is that students will find something at the right level to suit their taste. Teachers with students of very high ability will perhaps consider a critique of newspaper style. A 'brainstorming' lesson on this particular news report can be an enjoyable exercise, allowing students to identify the grammatical and stylistic weaknesses that characterise writing of this kind. ('Brainstorming' will be discussed more fully in the ensuing chapter on oral English.)

Traditional assignments on newspapers and other media are the hoary chestnuts of the trade, but nonetheless worthwhile stimuli for comprehensive practical activities such as the production of newspapers and oral work. So in a lesson comprising several disparate activities, an enthusiastic and committed group might choose to ignore the printed possibilities in favour of a more ambitious proposition such as arranging a visit to a local newspaper, interviewing reporters and editorial staff, and reporting on the workings of the newspaper trade. Whilst it might be possible to arrange for a whole class visit to a newspaper, the logistics are such that many teachers would hesitate at the prospect. A group of four or five students can engage itself far better without teacher presence. Needless to say, in the end it comes down to a knowledge of our students!

The integrated nature of GCSE suggests that the language coursework ought to reflect the use of a literary stimulus, in the form of either an assignment based on a single work of literature, or on a theme incorporating several different literary genres. Whilst some of the assignments suggested here might involve reading both of fictional and non-fictional English, an assignment sequence with a decidedly literary bias will have a broad appeal and serve to foster enjoyment in reading for its own sake.

There is no shortage of appropriate works for the single-text approach. The following assignment employs a work of literature that must surely be on the shelves of most English stock rooms.

GCSE Language Assignment: *To Kill a Mockingbird* by Harper Lee

Stage one

Having read the novel, choose one or more of the following sections. You may select whatever topics you wish within each section.

1. The Boo Radley story.
2. Childhood and growing up.
3. Racism.
4. Outsiders.

Stage two

1. The Boo Radley story

a) Read again the parts of the novel concerning Boo Radley.
b) Discuss the behaviour of Boo's brother and Nathan Radley in imprisoning Boo in his own home. Consider modern ways of dealing with young offenders, and suggest how Boo might have been treated today.
c) Attempt one of the following pieces of writing (you may choose another not printed here if you consult with your teacher first):
   i) Write either a diary or an autobiography as if you are Boo Radley.
   ii) Write a story about a part of Boo Radley's life in confinement.
   iii) Write a psychologist's report on Boo Radley, considering as many aspects of his behaviour as you can find in the novel, and make recommendations for his future treatment.
   iv) Write a letter from Boo to Scout in which you attempt to make friends and to overcome Scout's obvious fear of you.

2. Childhood and growing up

a) Read again those parts of the novel which reveal the various experiences of children at home, at school and at play.
b) Discuss some of the things that Jem, Scout and Dill get up to, and tell each other about your own experiences of this kind.
c) i) Write a part of your autobiography, bringing to life, as Scout does, memorable occasions. (Bring out your feelings and thoughts.)
   ii) Write about a part of the novel as if you were Jem.
   iii) Write a story about a child's first experience of school.
   iv) Write two views of Scout, one by her class teacher and one by Atticus.

d) Read for pleasure *Granddad with Snails*, by Michael Baldwin, or *Joby* by Stan Barstow, or *Cider with Rosie* by Laurie Lee.

3. Racism

a) Compile as full a list as you can of all the occasions in the novel when you think racism is revealed.

b) Produce two newspaper front pages for Maycomb, one by the white community, the other by the black, covering the events connected with the trial of Tom Robinson.

c) *Either* produce a poster condemning racism, *or* design and produce a board game which might help to emphasise racial equality.

d) i) Write a story in which racism plays a part.
   ii) In what ways is our society affected by racism today? Suggest how we should deal with the problems of racism in order to bring about a happier relationship between people of different races.
   iii) You are Tom. Write about your experiences, thoughts and feelings up to the moment when you are found guilty in court.

e) i) Study the main characters of the courtroom drama in the trial of Tom Robinson. By means of a group brainstorming session, decide on the personalities of each character, their attitudes and motives, and how honest and reliable each is. Then identify the key facts of the case as presented by both the defence and the prosecution.
   ii) Enact the courtroom scene as a role play, following the case as it happens in the book, or changing it as you wish. The verdict may be different too.
   iii) Improvise a *Panorama/World in Action* documentary following the trial, in which the programme host interviews various participants in the case.

f) Read and write a review of one or more of the following books which are about the topic of race and prejudice:
Ashley, B., *The Trouble with Donovan Croft*
Bowles, S. (Ed.), *A Question of Blood*
Braithwaite, E.R., *To Sir With Love*
Dhondy, F., *East End at Your Feet*
Guy, R., *The Friends*
Lingard, J., *Across the Barricades*
Needle, J., *A Sense of Shame and Other Stories, My Mate Shofiq*
Smith, R., *Sumitra's Story*
Wright, R., *Black Boy*

4. Outsiders

a) i) In small groups, decide which characters in this novel might be considered 'outsiders', out of step with the rest of society. Work out what these characters have in common and why they are in some way alienated.
   ii) Discuss either as a full class, or in small groups. What makes people outsiders in our society – in class, in school, in community.

b) Ask your teacher for permission to browse through the poetry anthologies in the stock room so that you can find poems about different outsiders. Using any poems that you can discover, as well as poetry that you have written, produce a poetry anthology on the theme of Outsiders.

c) Find out by whatever methods you wish as much as you can about what is done in your area to help people such as tramps and travellers.

d) i) Write a play about someone who is alienated from the rest of society.
   ii) Report on your findings in (c) in written form.
   iii) Choose from your reading in this assignment any character who is an outsider. Write a realistic diary covering several days in the life of this person.
   iv) Write about a day in the life of the Ewells, using whatever information you can find about their circumstances in *To Kill a Mockingbird.*

e) Read Barry Hines' novel *A Kestrel for a Knave*, the poem 'In the Snack Bar' by Edwin Morgan, and the play *A Taste of Honey* by Shelagh Delaney. Talk about your reading to your teacher or a small group.

Overview

This assignment is not intended to be prescriptive. Its suggestions for further reading could well be adjusted to accommodate the stock available in the English department and the school library. By making use of a selection of themes (the number of which could easily be increased), students can negotiate their own course of study, with only one prescriptive element: their final assignment profile must contain evidence of work in reading, writing and talking/listening. Any parts of the work achieved that are to be submitted for final assessment can be recorded clearly, alongside other contributions that constitute the ordinary business of interesting English lessons. Such a profile can furnish evidence of the ways by which assessment objectives have been met without necessarily offering every single task undertaken by the student, who will therefore feel free to experiment and to make a personal selection for final submission. As in other assignments included here, students can offer alternatives both before and after their work is completed. They can provide for us the most effective objective judgement on the material covered.

The topic of racism is a sensitive one that teachers may well consider difficult to deal with; its value is nevertheless significant, especially in all-white schools where prejudices may be well entrenched. Britain is a multi-cultural society which increasingly demands our acceptance of ethnic variety; for this reason an assessment course in English ought to include topics that will reduce the degree of discrimination and influence attitudes. This particular novel is ideal for delicate enquiry into the matter of racial prejudice, since it initially distances the subject in both time and place. The injustices within the novel are usually readily acknowledged by students, who might not be so unbiased about parallel circumstances in present-day Britain.

The use of a literary text as the basis of a language assignment is nothing new; thematic grouping of different literary genres is fundamental to much teaching and to many textbooks. However, whilst the GCSE course in literature might expect work which demonstrates a firm grasp of the detail of the text, together with understanding of themes and ideas, characters and authorial methods, the language course is entirely free from such restrictions. It does not matter that a student perverts the reality of the book's world to suit his or her own creative ends; in fact, the transformation of events in a story is evidence of original thought and valuable experimentation. Boo Radley, for example, need not be treated with the sympathetic eye of Harper Lee; Scout's first lesson can be viewed quite differently to display the character and behaviour of a disruptive pupil. To desire a rigid adherence to the literary evidence is to prevent much exciting talk and writing that engages students in active comprehension of abstract ideas as opposed to the finite understanding of the meaning of the text.

There is a danger that much comprehension of the kind set for examination will narrow responses. For purely assessment purposes, we might well wish to test students' understanding of the meanings of particular words and phrases, as well as their implications, but course work should avoid too much emphasis on what we think students *ought* to know. Once the interest is generated, students will gain far greater familiarity with the text by messing around with it than by concentrating on a tiny passage with a series of engineered and often arbitrary questions.

VARYING THE APPROACHES

Brainstorming

The examples of students' personal brainstorming of particular topics (Figs 2 and 3), one on the theme of conflict (a theme which might well have been included in the assignment sequence), and the other on a picture by Brueghel, illustrate how students can be given complete freedom to select what interests them rather than what we consider important. Released from worries about grammatical accuracy and spelling, a student can fill a sheet with pictures, cartoons, arrows and relevant written details which all reveal very clearly how much he or she really appreciates. In some cases the workings of a student's mind are extremely obvious. Of most interest, however, is the fact that various misunderstandings are outweighed by many valid views that a teacher might not have considered.

Non-literary Stimuli

The coursework folder also needs to reflect work done in response to audio-visual, pictorial and diagrammatic stimuli.

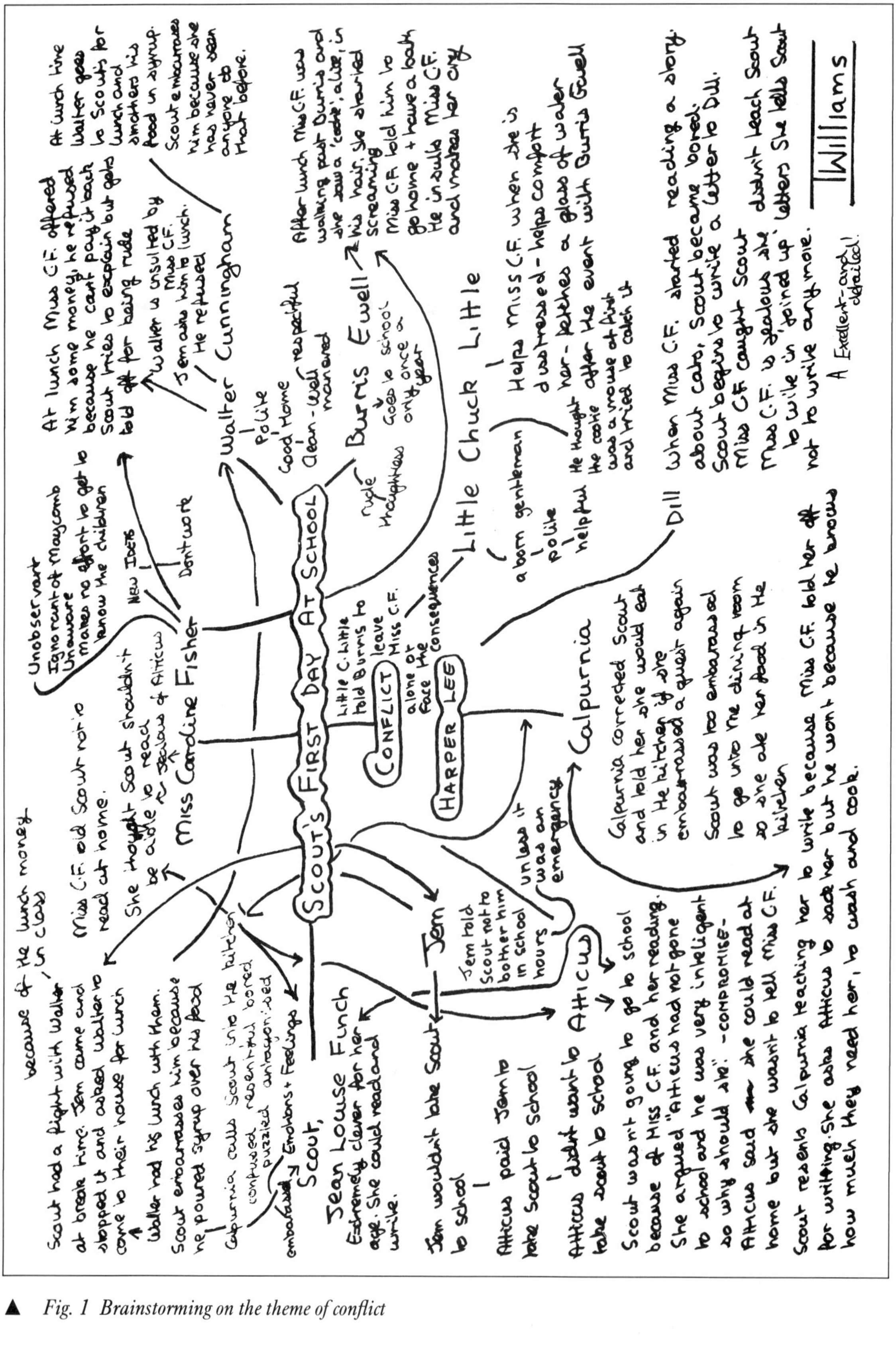

▲ *Fig. 1 Brainstorming on the theme of conflict*

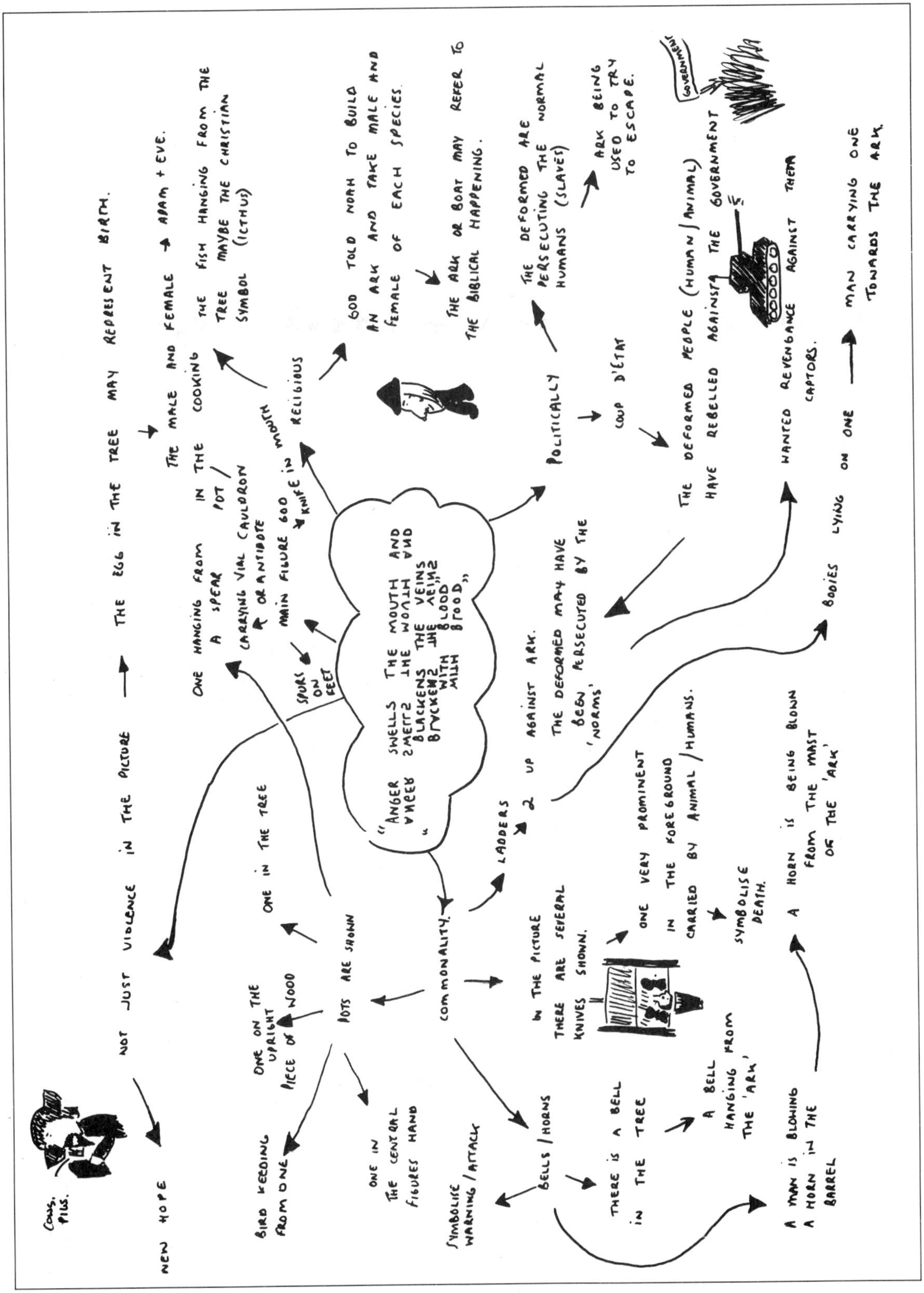

▲ *Fig. 2 Brainstorming on a picture by Brueghel.*
Both examples show that students' personal brainstorming gives them freedom to select what interests them, rather than what we consider important.

The possibilities here are unlimited, especially since the other academic subjects pursued by students are such a rich source of appropriate material at an appropriate level. Using language in a closed factual context is a particularly demanding exercise, as any class work on definitions will show; yet many students display a remarkable facility in such a language usage when they are on familiar ground. Likewise, if students can be encouraged to make use of knowledge and skills that they possess outside the 'English' curriculum, they are likely to realise the value of such linguistic expertise and transfer it readily to other contexts.

Individual members of a class might select a written task from a very broad range of possibilities: a student following a motor-craft course will, under controlled conditions in the English classroom, without any stimulus material other than acquired knowledge, produce coherent and technical accounts of the workings of the internal combustion engine or the braking system; the same student may find the discussion of a character in literature very hard to do successfully. Another student, working from an Ordnance Survey map, will describe a landscape and assess the advantages and disadvantages of certain locations from the point of view of a fictional house-buyer. A memorable example of good writing as a response to factual knowledge (in this case, of a piece of machinery) is included below. The task was to describe and show the workings of a piece of machinery of the student's own choice.

The turntable

Poetry in motion! Well, I must admit that it is a slightly biased statement in view of my general partiality for High Fidelity Equipment. Yet I think this is a perfectly reasonable point when applied to 'decent' turntables. A 'cheap and cheerful' (generally Japanese) turntable can be one of the most horrible, degrading and utterly repugnant pieces of equipment imaginable, yet a properly thought-out and built item is arguably the most important and certainly the most graceful device in the music reproduction 'chain'. What is so graceful about it is, really, patently obvious: it consists merely of a circular platter, sitting on a solid base, that revolves smoothly and evenly at a set speed. Its being the most important item of stereo equipment, however, is an area of rather greater contention. I, myself, am quite a 'vinyl' supporter, i.e., I believe records to be the overall 'best' medium for sound reproduction. As a medium it has an enormous range, fair durability, and an immense performance potential. Despite the recent onslaught of compact discs, vinyl has proven itself as, still, the most cost-effective solution, whilst remaining capable of superb quality with good ancillary equipment.

The turntable's importance is based on the idea that it provides the initial source of energy for which the other components are merely modulators: the turntable drives the record groove which vibrates the stylus, whose movements are converted to electrical impulses by the cartridge magnets and coil. This signal is then amplified and converted back into sound waves by the loudspeaker cones.

Hence, if the turntable is faulty, the signal can never be rectified, only distorted even more.

The turntable itself is generally (excepting the aforementioned overseas products) designed around the 'simpler the better' principle. Thus a quality motor unit (i.e. lacking arm and cartridge) which could set you back up to £8950 (to be honest, this is really a one-off case, more usually the maximum is about £2000) consists of a base, a platter, a motor, and some system of isolation from vibration.

The base is usually made from some vibration-absorbing or 'dead' material to attempt to isolate extraneous minor vibrations. In cheaper turntables this is usually wood or Medite (a synthetic dampened material), extending to marble, slate and solid steel in more expensive models.

Bolted to this base is a motor. This is normally a 'stable' DC motor which runs on a constant, smooth power supply. Cheaper units use synchronous AC motors which are synchronised with the 'pulse' in AC current, to allow smoother running. The power of this motor is transferred via an adjustable pulley (for the two speeds) and, usually, an elastic belt to the platter.

The platter is the round, twelve-inch-diameter support for the record itself. Again this is made of a sonically 'dead' material to avoid transmitting vibrations. It is covered with a mat of rubber or felt to avoid scratching the record and prevent slippage. The platter is supported by a central pinion set in a set of bearings in the base, to allow smooth rotation.

To top off all this 'anti-vibration' mania, the base is usually divided into two sections with springs and rubber damping between them. The most common system is the 'suspended subchassis', where a tripedal subchassis to which the motor, armboard (i.e. the plate onto which the arm is bolted) and platter is connected, is suspended, on springs, from an outer (wooden or steel) base. This way the springs act as shock absorbers for the actual record-playing equipment. Again, less expensive models may have other methods, using large rubber feet, for example, yet, as always, you get what you pay for and the most efficient system yet devised (used on the Goldmund Reference turntable aforementioned retail price of £8950) consists of a forty-kilo steel tripod, spring-mounted on an integral table!

Overall, in fact, turntable design is all about applying simple, basic engineering theory to its best advantage and, so as to avoid leaving you wondering, I shall round off with a few details of what may be termed the result of taking all this theory to its logical conclusion!

The Goldmund Reference:
Base – a steel, open frame table with spiked feet for vibration damping.
Motor – DC, infinitely variable speed controls.
Platter – 35 pounds, copper-sandwiched (copper has very similar vibration qualities to vinyl itself).
Subchassis – 40 kilograms, solid steel, tripedal with a spirit level in each of the 'feet'.
Total weight – 100 kilograms.
Total price – £8950 (excluding arm and cartridge!)

At the end of it all, however, it is 'only' a record player!

So, a coursework file is very much in the hands of the student; our job as teachers is to ensure that the course *as a whole* provides the widest possible range of writing experiences to meet the assessment objectives.

PREPARING FOR ASSESSMENT

Another consideration of teachers in the management of coursework is the encouragement of redrafting and revision of first attempts. Undoubtedly individual and group brainstorming is an effective way of instilling into students the value of redrafting without their even being particularly aware that that is what they are doing. Flow charts, diagrams and pictures generated by group discussion and individual thought are, in effect, the first draft which allows teacher intervention without infringing upon the rules of examinations, since no properly formulated writing has so far been achieved. In any case, the nature of assistance given is stated clearly in the record of work submitted to the board. If, after this initial planning stage, students are made clearly aware that no further help will be given, but that a first continuous piece of written work will in all probability have refined out neither the mechanical and syntactical errors, nor the inadequacies of the overall structure and paragraphing, most students are prepared to rework the original into a more finished form.

The marking of coursework is for some a problem (see Figure 4). Work produced in the very early stages of the course is often far inferior to that submitted later. To assess it according to final standards can result in both dissatisfaction and a lowering of morale. On the other hand, to give a false impression of a student's ability can cause later dismay. On balance it is probably better to be realistic from the start and to provide examples of work previously done by other candidates in order to establish a working knowledge of the possible levels of attainment. Even better is the ploy of bringing in some of the previous year's candidates with their coursework files to demonstrate both what can be achieved and what degree of development and progress is possible over a two-year course.

Students' identification of work to be offered as final assessment is also important. In a fairly lengthy sequence of work there might be quite a large proportion which for one reason or another is not particularly suitable for assessment, but has been part of the teaching/learning process. Students need to recognise this from the start and decide for themselves on which pieces they wish to spend most time and care.

Once the assessment pieces have been isolated, teachers will then mark according to grade criteria as defined in syllabus documents. Many teachers have found that to mark an impression best copes with the trade-off between one skill and another. We certainly find ourselves able to decide which area of the grade scale is appropriate for individual essays. Subsequent

▲ *Fig. 3 The marking of coursework is for some a problem*

adjustments will automatically occur in the standardisation process.

Of rather greater concern is our awareness of the range of different kinds of writing attempted by a candidate and submitted in the final file. The syllabus for each board prescribes the nature of final submissions, and the balance of personal, narrative, descriptive, argumentative or informative writing, and what is written in response to literature. It will certainly demand both careful record-keeping and attentive scrutiny to ensure that syllabus requirements are met.

EXAMINATION ASSESSMENT

The nature of the examination papers provided by the examination groups is, of course, determined by the overall scheme of a particular syllabus. The specimen papers available cover both 'closed' and 'open' kinds of writing, comprehension of a literary passage or passages, and understanding of and response to stimulus material of a factual kind presented in a variety of forms. Though it is beyond the scope of this book to provide a detailed critical analysis of the papers, they vary sufficiently to make desirable some comparison and appraisal of their main features, as our choice of syllabus will be greatly affected by them.

The presentation of stimulus in pictorial, statistical or diagrammatic form lends itself extremely well to external examination. The two boards which offer such papers are the MEG (Syllabus B) and the SEG (in both Syllabus A and Syllabus C). Of these two boards, the MEG has much more choice for candidates and is thereby much more attuned to GCSE thinking. Whilst the SEG paper for Syllabus A specifies as closed writing tests the production of both a letter and a newspaper article, the MEG requires one exercise of this nature (viz. letter, leaflet, speech) out of a choice of four.

Another significant variation is in the presentation of the tasks set: the SEG controls the context for writing by identifying in considerable detail the role and circumstances of the fictional letter-writer and the newspaper reporter; in the MEG paper, however, candidates must show more creativity in their definition of the imaginery writer's attitudes and purposes. This latter approach would be much more likely to stimulate candidates and to discriminate well between their performance. The presence on this paper of a written analytical account (of the three Chunnel proposals, represented pictorially) and of a sequencing and summarising exercise (based on seven disordered paragraphs from a newspaper) certainly makes the whole section a challenge to the most able whilst not preventing the weak from having a reasonable attempt.

The NEA have chosen coursework as the vehicle for factual writing; the LEAG, on the other hand, proposes to rotate the kinds of material and the styles of response, so that on some occasions data or pictures will be used, even though the specimen is of a literary kind.

Literary passages are common to all the specimen papers available at the time of writing (SEG Syllabus A, Syllabus C; LEAG Paper 2; NEA Syllabus A; MEG Syllabus B). Open-ended questions are frequently adopted, with heavy mark weightings; whilst these are accessible to the entire ability range, with results differentiated by outcome, they are a disadvantage to some candidates whose understanding is very good indeed but who fare badly because they are uncertain as to how far to develop their answers (the LEAG's rubric, stating merely that 'the five questions carry equal marks', is particularly unhelpful in its failure to indicate just how much candidates should be offering). Alternatively, some questions on the extracts are designed to elicit an imaginary/creative response directly related to the passage (perhaps as written by one of the characters) or about some parallel topic, linked by theme. In effect, there is nothing remarkably innovative in the kinds of literary comprehension on offer, but there are some noteworthy comments in the accompanying marking guidelines:

> The following marking scheme is not intended to be prescriptive and will be amended in the light of all positive achievements of the candidates. (SEG)

> A proportion of the marks will be awarded for literal understanding and recognition of what is explicitly stated. Additional marks will be awarded for development of ideas and recognition of what is implicit. (MEG)

> Points are set out in fine detail for the first three questions to show the abundance of relevant material, but candidates would not be expected to include all these points to gain full marks. A typical good answer would be one in which six or so central details were grasped exactly and organised into a coherent fluent answer, accurately expressed. (LEAG)

The variety of attitudes to marking reflected in these remarks suggests what we have commented on earlier: the boards are earnestly seeking ways to apply differentiation, but it is impossible at this stage to assess either the likely impact of a particular examination style or the effectiveness of the differentiation involved; the LEAGs final 'note' on its specimen paper sums it up:

> The rigour of this paper and the way in which it discriminates between omission depend on the level of response of a candidate rather than the nature of the questions.

This tacitly indicates that mark schemes in English are at best only guides to possible candidate response and that rigid adherence to a pre-agreed range of examples is impossible. It may prove that the examiner's scrutiny of exemplar material will be the only fair way of dealing with papers that test understanding.

Close analysis of the specimen papers really does confirm the inadequacy of the formal examination. The pitfalls to candidates of whatever ability have always been obvious; in addition, the need to spend valuable time working on examination 'technique' can be frustrating for us; passages selected can be less than stimulating; questions often do not lead the candidate towards any worthwhile conclusion, being simply for examination assessment; questions can be at worst sterile and at best fairly prosaic. With coursework, comprehension can at least be incorporated into a wider scheme of things: a candidate's true capacity for understanding is measured best by a context in which he or she really *wants* to know. Unfortunately, however well presented, the examination comprehension is a 'one-off' affair and as such unlikely to inspire candidates beyond what the incentive to gain a creditable grade encourages them to feel!

Another advantage of coursework comprehension over the

examination tests of understanding is that different tasks can be undertaken by students according to their ability; it is surely easier to achieve differentiation by this means than by weakening the potentially rewarding test by expecting it to cater for the full ability range. Since it is commonly accepted that there is a scale of difficulty inherent in the various comprehension skills (i.e. questions that seek evaluation and inference are more demanding than literal responses to the text), very able candidates can benefit more from a test of understanding that is not merely open-ended, but is both specific and searching. Likewise, the less able need more precise definition of what is required of them; they can be capable of good insights if there is sufficient direction.

At this stage it is perhaps best to conclude that the examination groups have had insufficient time to get their house in order (the NEA sample paper contains a passage and questions set for a previous 16+ examination!) and that the papers for examination in 1988 will have improved considerably on the specimens produced to meet initial demands for guidance.

4 Oral English

ASSESSMENT

How do we assess oral English? Achieving anything like reliability of assessment seems an unattainable ideal to anyone who stops for a moment to think of the complexity of spoken communication. Many teachers have declared that the impossibility of establishing common oral assessment tests that do not inhibit the candidate or produce a false estimation of ability in speech renders the whole idea of oral assessment a nonsense. If wide discrepancies exist between the assessments made by teachers in an individual centre, how on earth is proper standardisation between centres to succeed? The standardising meetings (referred to in the GCSE English *Guide*, p. 41) arranged by examination groups are supposed to be able to 'provide essential experience of the range of attainment that can be expected on given tasks', but will these be so limited in their range of application that they fail to accommodate the innumerable possible contexts within which assessment can take place? Fortunately research into oracy has at least enlightened current thinking about what elements of oral work can be considered for assessment, though it will perhaps be some time before all the examination groups can relinquish their notions of fine distinctions and acknowledge that good teachers of English can discriminate well between candidates without the massive encumbrance of elaborate assessment mechanisms.

Given a working knowledge of the grade criteria, as well as a sense of the need for positive assessment, most teachers will have a shrewd idea of the respective oral merits of their students from daily classroom activity. Regardless of criterion-referenced judgements, there is still going to be a temptation to evaluate oral achievement on a norm-referenced basis, with preconceived notions of what constitutes above-average, average and below-average performance, and with invidious comparison of student with student. We must resist that temptation; what we need to be most aware of is the versatility of each student in spoken communication: at the highest level, students are sufficiently versatile to cope well in a very wide range of contexts and registers; at the lowest, students might perform capably in one or two situations, but not be able to transfer their skill easily to deal with different circumstances. Our job will be to seek reasonable parity of standards along these lines, whilst rewarding positive achievement at all levels.

Survey of Examination Groups

The NEA is possibly the most enlightened of the groups in its expectations both of teachers and students. It stresses the importance of 'a whole variety of tasks with equally varied demands on [students'] oral ability' and offers a list of broad areas of ability:

a) to present and talk about information, imaginative work and what is read;
b) to select and evaluate evidence and present a point of view;
c) to discuss opinions or points of view;
d) to listen to others contributing and respond, showing understanding and appreciation of what is said;
e) to describe and communicate what has been experienced, felt or imagined;
f) to interact with others and respond appropriately in different contexts.

(NEA Syllabus A, pp. 19–20)

This particular examination group has implied that teachers are to be allowed tremendous flexibility, and freedom to create opportunities for listening and talking that are properly integrated into the other elements of coursework.

The MEG similarly avoids prescription, but requires assessment in five different speech situations. Slightly more control is exerted by the SEG in its requirement that all candidates must be assessed in three separate contexts, viz. pair work, group work and individual work. A mark for each context is to be submitted.

The London and East Anglian Group, with its oral 'test', consisting of 'discussions which develop from short talks given by members of a group in turn' (LEAG Syllabus, p. 14) gives a clear indication of reluctance to allow that teachers are better placed to determine the nature of contexts for assessment and implies that coursework assessments might be so unreliable as to warrant as controlled an examination of spoken English as this seems to be. The presence of a 'group teacher' to be a part of the circle of candidates, able to 'encourage the reticent and restrain the garrulous', is a sure way to create the most sterile and unrealistic presentation of students' language ability. A second teacher/examiner must watch and assess from the wings. The examiners fondly hope that such an informal layout 'should help to put candidates at their ease'!

This particular test is so unwieldy in its organisation that it will effectively eat away a sizeable proportion of the limited time available to us in the course. When is it to be conducted? The syllabus specifies that the examination of five candidates will take 45 minutes. Some schools have upwards of 250 candidates! Centres which have few candidates and which have blocked timetable arrangements for English may find it workable, if time-consuming, but otherwise it will entail extensive substitution complications or sessions out of school time, since two members of staff must participate. It is to be hoped that such a perpetuation of what is pointless and inadequate as a true estimate of students' ability in speech will shortly fail under competition from the other examination groups. This determination to assess under very controlled conditions flies in the face of the Bullock Report's criticism of the contrived nature of such exercises, which neither guarantee a reliable estimation of oral expertise nor accept the fact that frequently they depend less on oral skill than on writing beforehand. This end-of-course performance in this case is worth 50 per cent of the oral assessment; the exercise might have some value in a better context, were it properly integrated into the coursework. Ought we not to be looking at how students use language to achieve other ends than a spoken test?

Product and Process

A pilot research project for the JMB conducted in 1984 and 1985 at the University of Leeds by Douglas and Dorothy Barnes, members of the University School of Education, local English advisers and teachers, underlined the difference between the 'product' (oral work done purely for itself as a final performance) and the 'process' (oral work which arises out of the engagement of students in other English activities and is employed as the vehicle for achieving other ends than an assessment in speech) of students' spoken language. The practice of teachers has for many years (and certainly since Bullock) tended towards the generation of suitable occasions for encouraging students to participate orally, not purely in the presentation of a product (a prepared talk, a read passage, etc.), but in role play and simulation games, in problem-solving, in group work generally. To suggest the superiority over contrived oral situations of any method of encouraging classroom talk that is entirely natural, and imposes neither psychological pressure upon the speaker nor an awareness of any assessment of the speech, is not to suggest that product activities are of no value; on the contrary, the incentive of such an occasion as a prepared talk to a group can result in the production of oral work of tremendously high calibre. As an assessment method it can provide a useful common comparative test. It is not, therefore, a question of whether one context for assessment is better than another but a recognition that each context has evaluative worth and can have a widely different impact upon the students involved in it.

Some examinations at 16+ have already contained an oral assessment. The NEA 16+ Syllabus A, for example, with its 20 per cent oral component, has required assessment of three oral situations: a prepared talk, a prepared reading and a group discussion. Although these have frequently resulted in speech of remarkable quality, they are a burden to conduct and, what is worse, they discriminate unfairly against some candidates, who have, because of their culture and status, not been encouraged to perform in this way, or who have natural reticence or are very nervous. Many a candidate has failed under such stressful testing circumstances to demonstrate the expertise which has been obvious to the class teacher during the ordinary course of lessons. Fortunately the GCSE enables selection of oral situations that can play to a candidate's strengths and avoid the embarrassment (and sometimes distress) that can result from exercises such as those just discussed.

Why Assess?

At this point, it might be pertinent to consider why we are assessing speech in the first place: the examinations which have not included oral assessments in the past have not given a fair estimation of the overall linguistic capability of students who are very good speakers but much less skilful on paper; employers are interested in an advance indication of an interview candidate's facility in speech; we should be encouraging a general awareness and acceptance of the importance of speech, when in the past written qualifications have been solely significant. More important is the fact that we should be training students for their life beyond school, so that they are fully-rounded adults who can be attuned to the nuances of language as well as to use it to achieve their own ends. What we assess ought to be directly relevant to the real world, not the narrow confines of a single examination. Most people use speech far more than writing; it should go without saying that this aspect of language should be encouraged more than any other in schools and colleges.

Our commitment to generating speech in the classroom and the assessment of talk ought therefore to move away from the product towards the process elements, or at least to be a fair balance of the two. There is a further interest: if we wish to play down the overt assessment in order to develop process activities, how can we at the same time sharpen students' subsequent critical perceptions of their talk so that improvement ensues?

Assessment Techniques

The *National Criteria – English* (para. 5.2) offer the following guidance: 'the interactive nature of listening and speaking cannot be demonstrated solely by reading aloud or delivering a talk' and 'the techniques of assessment selected must require the candidates to perform a variety of tasks in a range of contexts' (para. 5.1). Together with the overall consideration of the integration of all the language skills, these guidelines should direct the planning of coursework as well as govern the means by which judgements are to be made about oral work. We should note particularly the attention drawn by the GCSE English *Guide* to the possibility of curriculum innovation in oral assessment (section 4.1, p. 36). However, rather than concern ourselves too much with the *Guide*'s recommendation that 'modest and attainable goals' should be set, we ought now to be making very clear to the examining groups what we deem important in our teaching towards oral work and persuading them to base assessment upon that.

The problem we have, in spite of our working knowledge of the merits of our students' spoken English, is how we can provide substantial proof of the reliability of our assessments, as well as to ensure comparability in judgements. First, as individuals and as whole departments we must identify for ourselves those skills which our coursework ought to test, so that they can be incorporated into the assignments that we create and thereby fulfil the national criteria requirement of a variety of tasks in a variety of contexts. As departments, we may find it helpful to isolate the most successful of our methods for stimulating oral work and abstract from them the key skills involved. Rather than plunging into a realm of untested and foreign methodology, we should rely upon our intuition as to what is best for us and capitalise upon that.

GROUP ORAL ACTIVITIES AND APPROACHES

Undoubtedly, small-group activities are the most productive of spontaneous involvement and the most democratic in their power to motivate individual students. At their most basic level, such as the joint reading of a play, the involvement of all members of a group is ensured. We would all acknowledge that a play-reading session is much more enjoyable for all members of a class if the class is divided up into several groups. The degree of participation exemplifies the power of small-group work to make the best use of available time, so that the maximum involvement of all students results. The small group can also handle the greatest number of communicative purposes; our task is to feed such groups with appropriate topics and ensure that each student speaks for as many different purposes as possible.

Most people's idea of a group discussion is the exploration of a single topic: school uniform; abortion; euthanasia; smoking, etc. The trouble with this sort of discussion is that it can discriminate unfairly against the student who is lacking in

▲ *The degree of participation exemplifies the power of small-group work*

relevant background knowledge (so that it is in fact testing general knowledge rather than oral ability) or is significantly weaker than his or her colleagues. The discussion is often sterile, being merely the regurgitation of received ideas rather than a positive interaction which actually develops. At best it can be rewarding both for participants and listeners; at worst it plods paradoxically quickly to a dead halt.

There are much better ways of exploiting small-group work. Role play, especially where drama is a powerful curricular force in a centre and students are therefore well-practised in such methods, can illustrate well the versatility of a candidate in meeting the demands of a multitude of hypothetical situations. As well as employing language in their own 'voice', students can experiment with the forms used by others, whilst at the same time interacting closely with their peers in a very natural and relaxed context. This particular method might arise *in vacuo*, or, better still, explore the circumstances of such an event as the assignment based on the street siege discussed in Chapter 3. The favourable impact of such an oral activity upon written work is well-known to English and drama teachers.

Problem-solving and simulation games likewise engender in students a real sense of involvement, with the resultant playing-down of self-conscious awareness that they are being assessed. One such game is included here in full, since, although with the advent of GCSE its subject matter is no longer relevant, its characteristics can easily be transferred to similar topics. It was devised by Stephen Clarke of the School of Education, University of Leeds, and has been successfully used with many students in recent 16+ oral assessments.

Six pupils are being considered by their respective English tutors for two available places in a GCE class. The rest must pursue CSE. The game provides a profile of each pupil, so that all participants can familiarise themselves with the characters and their abilities before the simulation begins. A headteacher has additional information to inject into this departmental meeting if such intervention seems necessary; this information is not supplied on the profiles given to the other 'teachers'.

Simulation game 'Fourth Form Transfer'

Headteacher's notes (Mr/Ms Joseph)

In front of you are the sets of information about six pupils, each 'profile' being written by an English teacher at your school. These pupils are at present in fourth-year mixed-ability classes for English, but they will have to go, after Christmas, either into a GCE O level English Literature class, or into a CSE set for their English examination. These six pupils: Jackie North, Robert Clegg, Susan Franks, Farida Akhtar, Peter Thatcher and Luther Freeman, are not easy cases to decide on, and so the English teachers are meeting in order to give each pupil's case a fair hearing before coming to a decision. You have invited yourself to the meeting and therefore don't want to say too much, beyond asking the occasional question. You have, however, views about each pupil and you are prepared to intervene and give your opinion in no uncertain terms if (and only if) the group of English teachers are about to make what you see as a big mistake. So, your task is to read this and then the six 'profiles' with notes attached for your eyes only. After that the discussion ought to begin, and you ought to be prepared to answer any questions that the English teachers ask you.

Setting the scene

[*Insert teacher's name here:* Mr/Ms P. Hartog, G. Sampson, G. Eliot, A. Bullock, J. Milton, M. Arnold.] You are an English teacher in a comprehensive school. Your work for today includes taking part in a discussion with other English teachers in order to sort out which pupils, at present in mixed-ability fourth year groups, will, after Christmas, go either into the CSE English set or the GCE O Level English Language set. All the pupils have been allocated easily enough and without discussion, but these last six cases are proving difficult. You have in front of you written details about those six pupils, and indeed you wrote the details about [*Insert pupil's name:* Luther Freeman, Peter Thatcher, Farida Akhtar, Susan Franks, Jackie North, Robert Clegg], whom you have taught, whilst the other teachers have written the other five. Your group must now decide which two pupils out of the set of six are to go into the O Level class, and which four into the CSE group. You must try to judge the suitability of each candidate on the evidence.

All that you know about the other pupils is what you read in front of you. The headteacher is also present at this meeting, and you suspect that s/he knows certain things about the pupils that are not mentioned in the profiles. The headteacher, however, is unlikely to say anything unless questioned, or, if s/he does speak, will only ask the occasional brief question.

To sum up: You should

i) read each profile in turn,
ii) ask any questions that you have of the headteacher,
iii) come to a decision in the group.

Profile 1 – Robert Clegg

Address: Lower Lane
Form: 4B.C.A.
D.O.B.: 16.10.70
Father's occupation: British Telecom engineer

Robert is a very untidy writer whose homework is often late and who has to be chased up to deliver it. However, the writing he does is sometimes original and shows that he has thought things out for himself. He can write stories that are funny and would win the examiner's approval on other grounds too, but the standard varies. In class he is very quiet – he seems to wait for other people to offer any ideas, but he does listen – if I press him hard enough, he will answer questions in a way that shows he has understood the ideas being discussed.

He's very vague about career ambitions – wants, perhaps, to go into the sixth form. He had an elder sister in the school who left two or three years ago (Claire) who was put in the CSE set and obtained a grade 3 pass. Robert says he doesn't mind which set he goes into, but, although more ambitious kids may want the O level places, I think that Robert should have one – if we put him into a top set he might be pleased to have the challenge. If he tries hard, he has it in him to succeed.

Signed:

M. Arnold

Headteacher
English Department teachers do not know that Robert's homework is often late and untidy because he spends time looking after a very sick mother. (His sister doesn't, apparently, care as much as he does.) He doesn't want anyone to know what he is up to and he doesn't want any favours from teachers. As his headteacher I have no strong feelings about which set he goes into, provided that he gets satisfaction out of his total programme of studies.

Profile 2 – Jackie North

Address: Topfringe Estate
Form: 4A.B.C.
D.O.B.: 15.10.70
Father's occupation: Personnel Manager of Technichips

Jackie's work in English is very tidily presented and is always handed in on time. In class she is attentive and seems to want to succeed. However, the quality of her essays and stories is dull, routine and full of spelling mistakes. If you outline in very close detail what to write, then she can manage, but she has very little individuality in her style of writing and she cannot, as some can, take a title and write about it usefully and at length. But, she is improving.

She is the youngest of three girls, all of whom are in the school. One, only a year older, is doing seven O levels and is confidently expected to pass at least five of them. The other, in the sixth form, is likely to gain a university place to study history. Jackie has always tended to lag behind her sisters, but her progress in the school so far has been promising; when she arrived, aged eleven, she could scarcely write at all and her reading was very poor also. Now she likes reading and enjoys discussions about books. She is anxious to get into the sixth form and get at least one A level. She needs, therefore, either an O level English pass or a CSE grade 1 pass. I think that she has become much better than she was at writing. The next two years (well, almost) should see a further improvement, and there is every chance that she will pass O level. With intensive practice at the right sort of essay she will get through.

Signed:

J. Milton

Headteacher
You think that J. Milton, who wrote this, is a bit soft on Jackie for the wrong reasons. She does indeed come from a respectable family, but you don't think that the description of her talents justifies the hopes placed in her. Her mother is very pushy and has, apparently successfully, been trying to persuade Mr/Ms Milton that Jackie is as clever as her sisters (which she isn't).

Profile 3 – Susan Franks

Address: Riding Lane
Form: 4A.B.C.
D.O.B.: 18.10.70
Father's occupation: Librarian

Susan Franks is a rather difficult case to decide on. If she went into the O level class she could well obtain a GCE pass in English Language. She works in a neat, tidy way and seems to like composing stories. The difficulty, however, surrounds her personality. She is so withdrawn, quiet and self-effacing that I feel she needs, for her own personal development, the benefit of our CSE course with its stress on a wide range of practical language activities such as group discussions, play readings and improvisations. These sorts of activities, as opposed to the GCE O level routine of essay-writing on your own and other exercises of a purely individual kind, might just enable her to find confidence. She could become more happy in herself and perhaps more able to face the world of work.

We shall need, of course, to persuade her parents that she is likely to gain a CSE grade 1, and we shall need to explain the position in a careful and tactful way to Susan herself.

Signed:

A. Bullock

Headteacher
You don't like the sound of this at all, but you don't want to make too much fuss if it can be avoided. If anyone asks you for your opinion about Susan Franks, you will make it plain that the girl should be in the O level set if she is clever enough, and that is all there is to it. If talk and playreading will help her gain confidence, then let those things happen in the O level class. Mr/Ms Bullock is fairly new to teaching and a bit uninformed about what goes on. Has s/he ever taught a GCE O level language class?

In any case, what Mr/Ms Bullock seems not to be aware of is that Susan Franks is quite chatty and sure of herself with other teachers. Furthermore, the English teacher whom Mr/Ms Bullock replaced rated Susan's O level chances as very high indeed.

Profile 4 – Farida Akhtar

Address: Vienna Place
Form: 4A.B.C.
D.O.B.: 17.10.70
Father's occupation: Textile worker

Farida arrived in England from Pakistan in 1976, and had not spoken English until then. She now speaks English very well, but does not use the language at all at home. I mention all this background because it has a bearing on Farida's case. Her written work is perfectly good except that, because of consistent small mistakes, it doesn't quite read like normal English. She tends, for example, to write 'in car' instead of 'in the car' and she doesn't always use sayings and English expressions with their correct meaning, even though she tries hard to include such expressions in her written work.

She wants very much, and despite her father's disapproval, to achieve a career in medicine, and she will not be able to do that unless she has obtained an English language pass or a CSE grade 1 in English. My feeling is that we could coach her to pass O level by lots of practice at likely kinds of essays – stories about family life, for example. She is, as is clear from the other subjects, a very bright pupil who simply needs more practice in the right kind of language. CSE would be less suitable for Farida because it would demand a greater range of styles of writing, continuously assessed work, oral work and so on, and it might not be, all of it, good enough for a grade 1.

Signed:

G. Eliot

Headteacher
You regard Farida as a model pupil, but you have two doubts. One is that others might be envious of Farida's place in the O level set in the one subject that she is known to be a bit weak at. You might ask Mr/Ms Eliot about how the other pupils would react in this situation.

In any case, there is a second doubt: Farida's father has already threatened to send her back to Pakistan unless she drops her career ambitions. You think it all too likely that he will carry out his threat, even before the examinations.

Profile 5 – Peter Thatcher

Address: Sebastopol Villas
Form: 4C.B.A.
D.O.B.: 19.10.70
Mother's occupation: Seamstress

There are some who would be affronted if Peter Thatcher were put in the top set without a debate. So, in the interests of a fair discussion, I include him among the 'problem' candidates. In fact, however, I think that his work is amongst the best.

I make no comment on whether the recent suspension of Peter has been of any help to him or to his teachers, but I do put on record that, for whatever inexplicable reason, this rebellious boy has always liked English and has worked hard for whoever has taught him that subject over the years. He reads avidly and can write accurate, detailed and often funny stories that would win any examiner's instant approval. He can always mimic anyone he meets, and, similarly, can imitate the style of many of the authors he reads.

The only question is whether or not he will be here in school for long enough to take the examination. I want him to remember school as a place where he could obtain at least some success, and he might just sober down if he thought that an O level pass or two might help him to a decent job.

Signed:

G. Sampson

Headteacher
You have great respect for G. Sampson's experience and views but you, like him, doubt whether this odd, unhappy and (for lots of subjects) ill-disciplined youth will stay out of trouble with the

police for long enough to have a go at the examination. Can you really allow such an unreliable pupil into a class for which good people are queueing up?

Profile 6 – Luther Freeman

Address: Corporation Row
Form: 4C.B.A.
D.O.B.: 20.10.70
Father's occupation: BR guard

Luther seems to be universally known and liked around the school, and not only on account of his prowess as a basketball player. His general attitude has been improving ever since he became good at sport and known for it. Fourth-year work has improved immensely and Luther can handle, better than most, the difficult business of writing conversation so that it reads exactly as if you were overhearing people talking. He also writes good song lyrics, when he can spell the words exactly as they sound rather than in their conventional English spelling.

One of the troubles with our present arrangements is that far too few of the black pupils end up in the O level sets. Putting the popular Luther into such a class, and making him work hard once he got there, could do much to encourage others, and it could go some way towards making the school a more just society. Luther will not automatically succeed. He has a considerable talent with words, but his spelling and punctuation are shaky and he insists on writing English more or less as he speaks it (except in the songs). However, surely we could persuade him to turn his gifts into a more standard and correct form for just long enough to pass the examination?

Signed:

P. Hartog

Headteacher
Luther, you agree, is a very pleasant pupil, but he's not a scholar and you don't believe he would pass even if he were given a place. Would it not be unfair to him to raise his hopes? In any case, despite your respect for the forthright expression of Ms/Mr Hartog's views, you are far from sure that a policy of counting which pupils of whichever colour are in which examination streams is at all helpful. Let the whole matter be determined by the usual factors – ability of pupils and availability of places.

Overview

Of the several virtues of this exercise, the best is its capacity to interest students and audience alike, regardless of their ability, since their familiarity with the issues at stake renders them all 'experts'. Once the game has been completed, the amount of further discussion of and challenge to the conclusions of the participants is rewarding and assessable! Because of their absorption in the exercise, students appear to forget completely that elements of their work are being assessed, and the 'process' talk in which they are involved well illustrates their abilities. Weaker candidates find the support of the printed profiles helpful, for although a fair proportion of their contribution tends

▲ *A good simulation game has the power to generate assessable 'process' talk as well as to interest students*

to be directly from the sheets, they can display some originality as a result of the ideas provided by the rest of the group.

There are other qualities: no one can be 'wrong', which alone guarantees that the experience is rewarding for everyone. The spirit of GCSE is implicit in this exercise's bolstering of self-esteem. As far as skills are concerned, students narrate (the best, in role, concoct anecdotes of their classroom experiences with these pupils), argue, listen to and consider information, express feelings, speculate, justify, explain, evaluate, persuade, and draw illustrations from real school life. The fact that they must place only two of the six in the GCE set ensures that there is a competitive element, but no animosity! Certain issues, such as racial prejudice or teacher bias, are handled without rancour and with a sensitivity that does credit to the linguistic prowess of the players.

Brainstorming

Reference has already been made to 'brainstorming' in the chapter on coursework. Simply described, it entails the provision of sheets of newsprint paper and plenty of felt-tipped pens, so that groups of four to six students can elect a scribe to note down anything and everything that members of the group might say. Any 'problem' can be set: in consideration of literature, students might be asked to select appropriate relevant material and comment on its use; a whole poem might be interpreted; a series of applications for a job might be scrutinised and compared; an advertisement or a newspaper article might be analysed for its content, style or significance. The opportunities are endless.

This method of making students talk works well. Protected by the single written record of all their comments, they are not afraid to voice their opinions and thoughts. The commitment

▲▼ *Brainstorming is a potent teaching/learning tool for generating oral and written work*

shown by all students is ample proof of its potency as a teaching/learning tool. Fortunately it can serve for assessment also. With weaker classes, whose members might be less well-motivated, there is for the teacher a written indication of the amount done, so that there is little chance of insufficient activity by the lazy! It is perfectly feasible for a teacher to observe and listen to each group in turn, recording the specific contributions by individuals. Though this entails obvious teacher activity towards assessment, students are usually too absorbed to be much concerned or adversely affected in their talk.

When the group session is complete, a representative from each group can report back to the whole class, whereupon whole class discussion may ensue. Certainly there is no difficulty in assessing such individual speakers. An advantage in this kind of solo 'performance' is that they usually show no signs of discomfiture, since they are not embarrassed about the content, which derives from several people rather than being a completely personal point of view; also, the supportive written material provides a useful structured stimulus from which to talk.

Taped Radio Programmes

Another type of group work that is particularly rewarding in terms both of its generation of talk and of opportunity for assessment of both product and process is the construction of a taped radio programme. Frequently employed as a means of developing students' awareness of their own oral calibre, this enjoyable activity incorporates a good deal of planning discussion as well as opportunity for criticism of self and others in the performance element. Like redrafts of written work, the repeated rehearsals of the various contributions emphasise well how improvement can be achieved. There is also the added advantage of assessment material that can be sampled by the moderator.

All of these group oral activities blend various language modes in a way that is entirely in keeping with the national criteria: they are truly interactive and require a high level of involvement by all students; they are reasonably modest in their time demands; they all lend themselves to objective assessment; they ensure that there is plenty of variation in the oral skills needed for their successful completion. All in all, they must constitute the most advantageous kind of approach to the testing of spoken language for GCSE.

INDIVIDUAL ORAL ACTIVITIES

Individual oral activities must still be central to an English scheme of work. If we are to test the true degree of versatility in language usage, we must find ways of overcoming in the most relaxed and natural fashion the inhibitions which afflict some students when involved in this most exposed of situations.

Solo Talks

Reporting back from a group discussion has already been mentioned. This, as we have seen, has supportive material and circumstances; it might, therefore, be worth considering how best to create solo assessment occasions which allow students to avail themselves of aids both to memory and to nerves! That most difficult of tests, the solo talk, is always better if the candidate has recourse to posters, printed material, drawings, slides, etc., or can use an overhead projector, which takes the spotlight off the speaker as well as giving visual stimulus to talk about. As we have already seen, however, this exercise must surely be optional and incorporated into a scheme of work that reduces the risk of a stilted performance.

Interviews

One-to-one 'interviews' of the kind exemplified on pages 42–3 of the GCSE English *Guide* can work even better if the candidate is talking to a peer rather than a teacher. Friends who are used to conversations on a casual basis are, in spite of the presence of a teacher assessing in the background, likely to perform well, their knowledge of each other helping to frame questions that best draw out the speaker being assessed. Like other group activities, pair work aimed at assessing an individual is best achieved with a specific task or problem-solving exercise. A student might be called upon to explain a diagram or a process; in the case of weaker abilities, to narrate from a series of pictures. Whatever the goal, the success of such a management of oral work will depend very much on the teacher's guidance beforehand.

Awareness of Purpose

As well as providing group and solo tasks, we should ensure that students explore and experience as wide a range of different communicative purposes as possible, and, wherever it can be managed, we should try to engender self-awareness of those purposes, in order to encourage the employment of peripheral skills that will enhance the prime aim of speaking. For example, a candidate might be helped to see how a narrative purpose might be enlivened by personal anecdote, humour, irony, pun, etc. Likewise, varying the audience is crucial to the successful improvement of spoken language. Reading stories to children (arrangements with local primary schools can easily be made) can give the narrative purpose a real context and call for techniques other than those employed in reading to a peer group or a teacher.

ASSESSMENT IN PRACTICE

Having come to terms with what we wish our students to do, we are then faced with the inevitable problems: how do we furnish the moderator with adequate evidence as to the work done and how do we achieve comparability of standards? We are all acutely aware of the dangers of the minefield that we are entering, and it would be foolish to suggest that there is a straightforward answer to our worries about fairness. Standardisation of oral tests of the kind employed by examination boards up to now has relied on video and live performances by students. These can be both helpful and entertaining; unfortunately they present product rather than process, which hardly helps us to acquire a satisfactory awareness of standards in the latter area. There is also some risk that, because of their limited range, they will be interpreted as examples of good practice and so inhibit the uncertain from experimenting widely with oral activities, for fear that boards' requirements will not be met.

More helpful are the internal sessions to which moderators come to appraise both the marking and the manner of conducting oral assessments. These occasions may be artificial, but show our own methodology and allow us to air our feelings as well as to influence board judgements over issues such as the assessment of student speech defects or dialects. There has always been concern over these; the general criteria thankfully support the notions of fairness in a linguistically and culturally diverse society; in the case of student handicaps in speech, it should be said that the exam groups seem prepared to entertain special consideration. (If in doubt, fight for it!)

External standardisation procedures will never be ideal; they will never be able to provide evidence of standards in every circumstance in which spoken English is used by our students; yet they must be seen to work, if only in part, for the credibility of the oral component of the GCSE to survive. It is to be hoped that compulsory elements are not imposed upon us by the examination groups in their determination to refute possible charges of inaccuracy in the final gradings; to prevent this we must not be afraid to declare our views about what is accessible to objective testing and we must avoid crying out for guidance from the boards when we should be guiding them!

Audio-visual Recordings

The worst that could happen to us would be the compulsory production of cassette recordings for every candidate: such a requirement would not, of course, be impossible to handle; we might just wonder, however, whether the whole course should be alternatively entitled 'Spoken English'! We ought to establish straight away the inadequacies of tapes as assessment material, though GCSE lends itself very well to the delights of recording for coursework activities. These are the practical problems. Are the recordings to be produced under supervision? In which case, can candidates be supplied with suitable places for the recordings to be made? (This rules out the classroom with the whole group present!) Do we have enough machines and cassettes for the whole department? Surely the 'massive' government funding for GCSE would be better spent on alternative resources, such as class reading boxes! Will the tape recorders work? If the tapes are done in students' own time without teacher supervision, can they be regarded as valid assessment material in view of possible malpractice? Is an audio-recording a fair indication of a candidate's work, when the visual support of paralinguistic elements is removed? Is the very fact of having to produce a recording detrimental to performance? (It is unusual for anyone to be unself-conscious when a microphone is switched on.) Is the random sampling by moderators of audio recordings likely to achieve any better results than the sampling of live performances? (The disproportionate amount of time that would be spent on taping would have to mean a very real advantage in the use of cassettes.) Haven't we got enough to do without listening to tape after tape in order to complete the gradings of student performance?

Audio-visual recordings, for the centres lucky enough to have good facilities, would perhaps suggest themselves as possible alternatives, but again the crucial questions of time and money, as well as the disadvantage of student self-consciousness, indicate insuperable barriers to an effective assessment system. Both audio and audio-visual methods find their true place in the more important aspects of student self-appraisal and learning. Seeing oneself or a classmate on video is a sure way of illustrating weaknesses and characteristic physical and linguistic traits; the enjoyment of filming and taping is also a real incentive to most students to active oral involvement. Student evaluation of the results must be the main benefit of such activities.

Checklists

Then there is the checklist approach. Various grids have been suggested for the assessment of spoken English. The NEA, MEG, and SEG have all included in their syllabus documents grids that are designed to record the spoken contributions of candidates. These vary in their demands upon the teacher.

The NEA does not insist on the use of grids, but offers two samples that teachers might wish to use. The first records a definition of the task, and then on one axis provides a list of names, whilst the other defines separate skills, such as presenting ideas, listening to and responding to and evaluating evidence. The disadvantage of this is that it offers room only for ticks, marks or grades and presupposes the teacher's ability to discriminate easily between the separate skills employed by respective students while a lively conversation is in progress. This particular grid is intended for the whole class on one occasion. The second NEA grid is designed as an individual student record of several occasions on which various skills are employed, one axis specifying the situation, the other the skills. Again the spaces available are relatively small, aimed at single marks or very short comments. This checklist is perhaps better than the other, since one sheet displays at a glance the overall achievement of one student; the other system would entail leafing through a series of sheets to ensure that all skills had been adequately tested.

The MEG version prescribes the recording of marks out of ten, the vertical axis of the grid showing the date of each of five different activities and the horizontal one stating the activity, the teacher's mark, written comments on performance and the moderator's mark. This is simple to complete, and perhaps reveals MEG's awareness of the burden of assessment which teachers will have to shoulder. Impression marks based upon the given grade descriptions will no doubt become more reliable with familiarity!

The SEG will employ two separate sheets, one for recording marks awarded for each of three different spoken situations (pair, group, individual) and the other for defining the tasks undertaken. No separate definition of particular skills is expected.

It is apparent from the syllabus evidence that the examination groups vary considerably in their expectations of what teachers can provide by way of proof and assessment in grid form. What

Vocabulary
Register
Listening
Delivery
Purpose
Intonation
Pace
Narrative
Reciprocity
Appropriateness
Content
Hmmm, now let me see . . .
Answering
Audience
Describing
Asking
Interpreting
Intelligibility
Collaborating
Arguing
Audibility
Persuading
Evaluating

▲ *Fig. 1*

we should hold uppermost is the value of the assessment method to our students! If the method is to be purely for assessment and not as an aid to student development, then we might consider Pauline Chater's grid (in *Marking and Assessment in English*, Methuen) which lists the following skills on one axis: content, delivery, appropriateness, reciprocity, ability to transmit ideas and feelings, to describe experience, to narrate, to present a point of view, to ask questions, to answer questions, to describe a process. A series of columns lists the separate oral occasions. Pauline Chater's method employs ticks to differentiate between a very able (two ticks) and a fair (one tick) performance, and a cross for weak responses. This method is simple and can be administered unobtrusively and easily by a teacher sitting alongside, for example, a group discussion. It has its limitations, however, since the list of skills is not comprehensive, and a comprehensive list would be unmanageable. The fact that students would probably not benefit from this grid (although teachers presumably would articulate their criticisms after a performance, since students derive considerable advantages from a written report) is another consideration. (One humorist at the Phase 2 training envisaged a student seeking guidance: 'Please, miss, how do I improve my reciprocity?')

Checklists can be helpful in a number of ways. They certainly can focus the teacher's attention; the awareness of particular skills can sharpen the perceptions of the assessor, who is able to identify positively the merits of a candidate's performance. Since we are in the business of giving positive messages to our students, this can be very supportive to a poor candidate who might be demoralised to receive a mark without any verbal qualification that outlines the good points. Another advantage of the checklist is that it is a useful reminder of the range of tasks set to meet the criteria, as well as of the variety of skills that students are called upon to demonstrate. With a department, checklists can help to achieve consistency of approach, especially in those centres where there are several non-specialist teachers trying to make sense of new methodology in two subjects. Probationers and students would also find reassurance in the presence of assessment grids which outline expected qualities of spoken language. Checklists can also save time in making assessments, since they can be fairly easily administered in class and impose no extra workload once a lesson is over. No doubt some of departmental capitation will find its way to the purchase of clipboards!

Diaries or Journals

Of all the possibilities so far suggested by research, the diary or journal seems the best in terms of its flexibility and overall value to student and teacher alike. One of the most important factors of all in determining the comparative spoken abilities of our students is a proper outline of the context in which they speak, a description of the stimuli, the communicative purpose, the audience, the reason for its taking place (the diagram on p. 38 of the English GCSE *Guide* provides a helpful summary of these aspects). However, because of the sheer number of possible speech contexts we may find it difficult ever to be able to compare like with like. Nevertheless, to establish clearly on paper the nature of the event will at least demonstrate what has been achieved as well as provide a point of reference as to the assessments made. In using a journal, we ought to be allowed to devise methods of recording that are suitable for our own needs and classroom practice. It may be that some teachers will prefer to allocate sections of an exercise book or a loose-leaf binder to each candidate, in which they can note down the distinguishing features of notable oral achievements by each student, while at the same time cross-referencing with a separate summary of the whole-class activity, where appropriate. Alternatively, a journal might on one page record all student contributions, with critical comments, as well as the nature of the work undertaken. A journal might contain purely written comments or marks as well, depending on the method adopted by the teacher.

The value to students of the journal means of record-keeping has already been suggested. Any way of drawing attention to weakness and limitations (not to mention the positive qualities of what students have done), whilst at the same time opening up opportunities for critical appraisal with a teacher, must engender a spirit of self-development that can only enhance future activities. Active student involvement in the assessment process can also be an incentive; if they keep their own diaries of oral work, the examiners will have a formidable display of evidence to sample, since far more occasions than could ever be created in class would be entered from students' lives outside school or college.

Applying Criteria

Having adopted the practice that best fits our needs, how do we apply the criteria offered for assessing oral work at each grade level by the board's syllabuses? The candidate performing at grade 1 level will be competent in the broadest range of skills in the broadest range of circumstances, being able in addition to demonstrate the ability to interact well with others, and managing complex language with flair and sense of occasion. The grade 5 candidate will operate at a much more simple level, able to respond in a limited way to group work and manage communication reasonably coherently on an individual basis, but will not have the flexibility looked for in better students. We should be realistic, too. Fifteen- and sixteen-year-olds should not be expected to match the rhetoric of Cicero or the gift of fluent and varied speech achieved by the Johnny Morrises and the Patrick Moores of this world. We should acknowledge that there is an unlimited hierarchy of excellence in speech above the top mark awarded; though we might enjoy the pleasure of spoken offerings by the occasional very gifted student, we should not fail to take account of compensating qualities in less-able candidates who still deserve a top grade. It is on this kind of issue that we shall find ourselves obliged to fight to justify our judgements, having recourse to good records which will help to substantiate our claims for the award of particular grades.

What we most need, therefore, is the clichéd 'courage of our convictions' in awarding oral marks and grades. The GCSE upholds the aspects of positive learning and positive experience for all students; from that position of strength we must argue forcibly in the case of doubtful or borderline candidates, remembering the degree of subjectivity in judgement which afflicts moderators just as much as teachers. We should aim for cooperation rather than mutual distrust in the dealings between centre and board; one thoroughly successful oral standardisation meeting recently sent back to their schools representatives happily reassured of their powers of discrimination simply because the presiding chief moderator acknowledged that subjectivity was inevitable and that variation in the awarding of grades would always occur. As teachers, we must accept the responsibility of making oral assessment work; we must also be *seen* to be making it work, too, or our credibility as assessors will be forever lost!

Value of Oral Work

Those who deny any necessity for oral assessment and who view the imposition of compulsory oral work with dismay should consider how influential its presence will be as an examinable element of English in achieving what the Bullock Report and 'Bullock Revisited' have both affirmed: that talk must enjoy an active share in the balance of work in the English classroom. The very fact that we are now obliged to assess spoken English will ensure that our perceptions as to what can and should be achieved will be sharpened, and our methodology improved. Our expertise in dealing with the examination of spoken English is a stepping-stone to the future creation of records of achievement; we might as well get it right straight away!

LANGUAGE ACROSS THE CURRICULUM

Apart from the general worth of English classroom practice of examining spoken language (though there will continue to be those who will sustain their staunch antagonism to it), the elusive 'language across the curriculum' may at last have a chance to flourish as an understood concept with a true value in all subject areas. Whatever we think of the perpetuation of the single-subject approach to which the GCSE seems absolutely committed, we can realistically expect for many years to come to face the challenge of injecting linguistic fervour into colleagues isolated by their own subject domains.

How do we do it and how is the GCSE structure going to help? First of all, we must recognise and capitalise upon the splendid array of potential speech opportunities in other

▲ *Fig. 2 An ideal to contemplate for oral assessment*

people's lessons. Having inculcated into our students the need for regular entries of oral work made in their personal journals, we should sell them the idea that English is not just for English lessons; this isn't so hard when the scientific Philistine who remains immune to our evangelical enthusiasms about talk about poetry, say, realises that what really does make him or her tick can be drummed into service for oral assessment. Chance a visit to a science lab, a cookery room, a modular technology seminar or a computer room, and what do we find? If not students' fanaticism, at least a total absorption in high-powered technical topics with language to match. If a student in one of these subjects can explain to a friend how to do something, coherently and clearly enough for the friend to understand, there is real communication going on in the most natural of circumstances. After a particularly trying time encouraging a low-ability fourth-form class to participate in group discussion, a colleague happened upon an outdoor motor-cycle mechanics lesson involving the same group of students. He was impelled to eavesdrop on some of the conversation; it wasn't inspired, but it was pertinent and reflected complete engagement in the subject. The students noticed him, of course, but very quickly ignored his presence; the irony of the situation, considering their previous lesson, passed them by!

So, there are opportunities, but they need to be tapped. We are hard pressed, as are teachers in other subjects, and the best way forward will be through our students, whose journals can be shown to other subject tutors, who may then appreciate what we are trying to do. The fact of coursework in other curricular areas ought to make staff sympathetic to our needs. Involving such colleagues as physics specialists in the assessment of speech may not at first seem a likely proposition, but they are no doubt very aware of the particular merits of their students in terms of explanation of experiments, for example, and might therefore be encouraged to comment, perhaps in written form, on student journals, or verbally in the staff room; an initialled validation of a student comment would do very well. If we can be involved in the event, that is all to the good. The more significant occasions when speech occurs will be recorded either way. It is helpful to mention to other subject tutors the chief criterion by which talk should be assessed: how far does the student succeed in communicating within a specific context? Does this talking do its job? Getting others to see a value in talk is the greatest gain; it may be that we shall need to find an inservice-training slot to achieve common understanding of this, but individual approaches will always fare better.

RESOURCES FOR ORAL ACTIVITIES

Once some sense of direction has been established, it will be the concern of English departments to develop a resource bank, perhaps card-indexed, of widely different oral activities that can be drawn upon by everyone, for inclusion in coursework sequences or as isolated tasks. Such ideas could well be grouped to facilitate access and to encourage future ideas along similar lines.

Surveys of local issues

These should include the following:

group discussion engaged upon choosing what to do;
deciding how to divide the task between participants;
conducting necessary research in order to produce suitable materials;
devising and administering questionnaires;
interviewing a range of people;
collating results;
presenting a summary of the topic.

B/TEC groups recently used this type of exercise to assess local parking needs, to investigate reaction to the introduction of a cafeteria system, and to discover public feelings about the teachers' industrial action. The combination of product and process elements enabled coordinators of the course to assess a range of different uses of language.

Printed stimuli for use at particular levels of ability

Foreign language papers have exploited this method of engaging students in narrative work, following a sequence of pictures. This kind of resource is valuable for weaker candidates in providing a secure and structured framework. There are plenty of other types of visual stimulus to choose from:

a sequence of pictures to illustrate a process (wiring a plug, changing a car wheel, replacing a broken part, etc.);
single pictures with plenty of detail;
a range of connected pictures (such as a series of human figures);
street plans.

Teachers will find various ways of using such material; students could be asked to give instructions for the completion of a task such as the drawing of a geometrical shape by a friend; small groups could look at pictures of people and express their opinions of personality and lifestyle. Stereotyping is an excellent topic for this method, especially if care is taken in the choice of pictures (policemen, punks, people of different race, children, old folks, etc.), since students can explore attitudes and challenge preconceived notions about groups in society.

Suggestions for ways of using audio-visual aids

A real task, such as a video film demonstrating how to use a school library, provides a tremendous challenge for abler candidates. This particular exercise, which will genuinely help young pupils entering a school, is ideal for its integration of speaking, reading and writing skills, not to mention presentation. The production of a suitable script entails detailed research into the workings of a library (classification systems, indexes, supplementary resources, etc.) as well as unlimited discussion of how to make use of the findings. Liaison with the librarian offers interviewing skills, whilst the 'acting' entails critical advice and appraisal as well as performance. (Long-term availability of a video camera is of course a pre-requisite!) Activities could include:

creation of slide-tape sequences;
audio-taped interviews;
audio-taped radio plays/programmes;
audio-video recordings of documentaries;
audio-video recordings of advertisements.

Problem-solving/discussion stimuli in printed form

Such resources find themselves in frequent use, whether they are fictional or real. The quoted example, 'Fourth Form Transfer', illustrates how supportive this kind of stimulus can be. Similar approaches might consider a range of application letters and biographical information, or present various views of proposed plans for, say, an airport runway extension or demolition of a building of historic interest. Drama specialists will readily provide plenty of useful topics!

Departments will inevitably choose what is feasible according to hardware resources, class sizes, staffing, rooms and so on; time will perhaps be the most potent influence over what we eventually succeed in doing. The implications of this will be considered in the following chapter.

5 GCSE Assessment and Records of Achievement

Where do we go from here? From 1988 we shall have established single-subject courses that confirm the entrenched view that the various components of the secondary school curriculum are disparate and autonomous. GCSE is an improvement, but it still does not address the issues of an integrated curricular pattern that would break down the barriers between subjects and rationalise school strategies. Furthermore, the developments in student profiling and the building of 'records of achievement' suggest a vigorous shift in emphasis that heralds a new phase of education; this may very well necessitate our absorbing into our current lesson allocation the task of appraising the cognitive aspects of students' learning as part of a much wider picture of their positive attainment.

SIMILARITIES

There are a number of parallels between the GCSE and profiling, perhaps the most striking of which is the value placed upon the 'process' of learning and of assessment as opposed to the 'product'. The chapters on coursework and oral English have drawn attention to the significance of continuously assessed skills which are crucial aspects of development; summative assessment may not reflect the true achievement of candidates, just as a summative profile may not do justice to the whole of a student's learning experience in secondary education.

The similarity between coursework and records of achievement goes further: we aim through the continuous assessment of students to enhance their rate of progress by giving them a greater responsibility and direction over the pattern of their studies; in other words, the assessed work becomes a teaching and learning mechanism rather than a mere recording of standards attained; likewise, in profiling, we are seeking to involve students in their own education with the aim of increasing their commitment and motivation. The final profile, containing a complete picture of a student's experience of every aspect of school life, academic and extra-curricular, as well as a good deal of supportive information about private interests and attainments, is ideally the product of an ongoing two- or three-year process of staff–student interaction and negotiation; the ideal course of study in an assessed subject such as GCSE English should enter upon an equally careful interrelationship of teacher and student, which will record the entire picture of cognitive development, and, unlike the final exam grade, offer to employers, parents and examiners a far more rounded representation of achievement.

If we assume that before very long we shall be required to contribute to records of achievement, we shall quickly recognise that the success of our endeavours will be directly related to the systems of record-keeping and reporting that we operate. In this most important of school subjects we still have a very powerful impact upon the final impression created by a student's profile. Our final mark or grade will not, perhaps, be as significant as our written presentation of a student's positive achievement in reading, writing, listening and speaking, the product of two years' painstaking encouragement and scrutiny of what our students do.

PRACTICAL REQUIREMENTS

What are the realities? Limited time, large classes and rigorous examination requirements are the norm in most schools. Add to that a fair proportion of disaffected young people who cannot settle to work, thereby wasting a disproportionate amount of lesson time, and we could readily conclude that this profiling business is a non-starter! Faced with these apparently insurmountable problems, we shall have to fight some curricular battles to give ourselves at least a reasonable chance of tackling the job successfully.

Timetabling

Our first priority could well be the provision of blocked timetables; schools with an eight-period day, blocked in doubles, have splendid advantages in terms of flexibility of staff and pupil arrangements. Being able to put classes together on joint exercises gives teachers a number of benefits, including the sharing of work schemes, streamlining of presentation of material, releasing one tutor for individual activity in, for example, oral work or student negotiation, and improving departmental cooperation and awareness of each other's teaching styles and methods. The presentation of topics by different members of staff can be stimulating and refreshing to students; the preparation time for individual staff can also be reduced. Failing the wholesale blocking of time, departments could well attempt to persuade timetablers to achieve parallel arrangements on a single-lesson basis, which would permit at least some integration of the various groups.

Classroom Organisation

Creating time within lessons is of paramount importance; consequently any bias towards teaching from the front will have to give way to a kind of classroom organisation with which some schools have long been familiar. Working from the foundation of existing student competence in language, through the medium of strategies such as brainstorming and small-group discussion, we open up opportunities for moving between students in a counselling, negotiating or assessing role. Desk arrangements are very much a personal matter; it is easy to advocate grouped desks, but success in teaching that way presupposes a particular kind of strategy that some teachers find impossible to embrace. However, since group work has to be done with appropriate furniture positions, flexible classroom organisation is a worthwhile aim. It is surprising how much time can be gained for more valuable tasks by giving students a greater power in the selection and pursuit of their own course of study. For one thing, if students are well motivated, and group work properly managed tends to make them so, they open up avenues for themselves that would not be explored in the whole-class approach.

Counselling

At least some of the weekly allocation of lessons should be made to create the circumstances that will allow us to interview students individually – not to mark work with them, but to discuss what choices are to be made (in, for example, the completion of an assignment), what personal interests can be taken up, what elements of a scheme of work are best selected for final assessment, and so on. Good counselling is vital (it is no use pretending that it is an easy skill to acquire), both for the effective use of available time and for ensuring that students have a fair crack of the whip. Negotiation is more than a teacher telling a student what to do! Some teachers may very well feel threatened by the prospect of diminishing control over what students are doing; their fear that some of their charges will simply take advantage of a freer system can be considerable. The answer lies in the structure of coursework that offers choice, but entails deadlines and has some inbuilt restrictions; students know that they must fulfil certain requirements and usually respond well to the availability of options. Weaker candidates can derive security from a closer adherence to printed assignment material, whilst the more able can avail themselves of whatever personal interpretations they may wish to make of it.

ASSIGNMENT PROFILES

Proper staff–student discussion of finished work is likely to be improved if students make a written appraisal of what they have done, providing information about what they have found difficult or easy, what drafting or correction they have attempted, what overall sense of satisfaction they have derived from the task and what specific details they see as being particularly successful. This may direct the teacher's attention to central issues and help to establish a positive critical message. It is helpful to know what a student values in his/her own work, since that enables the teacher to create initially a general air of agreement against which negative criticism can profitably be made, without fear of damning out of hand what the student feels proud of! A 'cover sheet' or assignment profile accounting for the various components of an assignment could well serve as this student record.

Not only does a record like this help students to organise their work systematically and indicate what has been completed and what is still to be done; it also allows them to tackle things in any order, according to their needs. For example, a research exercise that cannot be carried out in class may be protracted; subsequent parts of the assignment can therefore be done first without wastage of time. Furthermore, a student in compiling such a cover sheet is very conscious of the quality of finished pieces, since a personal account is to be submitted. Students are generally well able to perceive their limitations, even if they don't always know how to correct them; their identification of particular areas of weakness is therefore a useful aid to the teacher working within severe time constraints.

Heads of department will now, with all the novelty of the GCSE criteria, be at pains to draw departmental practice into a more structured framework than has been necessary in the past. Any method of record-keeping will have to be accepted as profitable by everyone as a learning device, as a gauge of teacher effectiveness, and for the dissemination of information about student progress to pastoral colleagues, heads and deputies, parents and employers; unless this is so, it will cause either extreme dissatisfaction amongst colleagues or simply fail to work at all. The cover sheet method has the prime virtue of being for the most part completed by students, while teachers can summarise in relatively few words the students' verbal and written commentary at the time of consulation, disagreeing, confirming or qualifying as appropriate. The product of this is a document relevant to a specific set of learning skills and objectives; by the end of the course, each student will have one for each assignment undertaken, with a precise account of the range of activities covered and an associated teacher comment and validation.

If students transfer the gist of teachers' criticisms of each separate element of a marked assignment to the profile sheet, a very comprehensive portrayal of the overall achievement is obtained for future use. This, of course, will furnish examiners with additional information that substantiates and enlarges upon the coursework record submitted by teachers, itself a means of ensuring that all the national criteria objectives are met by the range of coursework assignments. By means of the assignment profiles, students are led to a developing awareness of how their reading, writing, listening and speaking are progressing, directing them to further practice in those skills which indicate the greatest need for improvement.

As has already been suggested, the design of each cover sheet will be dependent upon the nature of the assignment it deals with. Though a truly mass-produced sheet for comprehensive departmental use sounds a good idea, in practice it becomes rapidly obsolete as recording systems themselves develop. No teacher of English wishes to be constrained by such a document – since every assignment is unique, not just to the department but to individual tutors, the associated record will arise naturally, tailored to suit the various tasks set. The provision of a skills checklist on the profile may also serve little purpose, unless it is devised purely for one assignment, in which case it can be extremely helpful, alongside other assignment checklists, in identifying the whole gamut of activities covered by the course. So, one assignment might demonstrate that a candidate can:

write a business letter;
paragraph correctly;
accurately compose and structure sentences;
read with fluency;
extract information from reference books;

while another might show a student's facility in:

writing imaginatively at length;
using a wide vocabulary;
writing fluently and accurately;
reading aloud with interest and fluency;
taking part in a group discussion;
listening and responding to the spoken ideas of others.

It is obvious enough that most students will respond actively to the stimulus provided by such information as these checklists which have been distributed before they tackle any of the work of an assignment.

All in all, the simpler the format of a sheet, the more likely it will be that staff will embrace it as a pertinent tool in assessment and in motivating students to take a much more active role in their education.

If we can accept that the orientation of assignment profiles towards student involvement will at least ease the reporting load, while classroom organisation can offer occasions for adequate one-to-one consultation, we are more than half-way to meeting the kinds of record-keeping that will be asked of us.

LIMITING ASSESSABLE COURSEWORK

The remaining factor in gaining that elusive time element must be related to the amount of examination assessment work set. On this issue, departmental accord may not always be easy to achieve. There will be those members of staff who resolutely pursue coursework through innumerable assignments, rendering the entire two years of the language course a treadmill of student assessment; other colleagues may attempt to complete coursework with a minimum number of assignments. However, members of the department must acknowledge that the relative balance of English Language and English Literature must be carefully worked out; it will also occur to colleagues that a unified attitude to the proportions of time allocated to examination and non-examination pursuits will assure everyone of the security of a common approach. An agreed limit to the number of coursework assignments has the beneficial effect of allowing students to 'take a breather', to pursue activities of their own choice and to acquire skills through the medium of personally-selected or teacher-proffered learning contexts that do not fit the mould of the syllabus requirements. Whether these are as particular as spelling programmes for needy individual candidates or as general as reading for pleasure, whether they are teacher-directed or taken up voluntarily by students, such interludes in the relentless movement towards final assessment are both necessary and desirable. Everyone's morale depends on it!

Limiting assessable coursework also defines the boundaries for the concomitant administrative needs; we shall have to create opportunities for doing these well, since much depends on them. This book has suggested no more than the concurrence of members of a department to conform to a predetermined pattern or blueprint for the construction of coursework assignments; it certainly does not recommend that everyone should do exactly the same! However, where there are close working arrangements within the department, there are also frequent opportunities for cross-marking, cross-fertilisation of ideas and strategies, and a comforting sense that we are heading in the right direction! Assignment profiles can also be validated by departmental colleagues where marking of each other's students takes place.

There will be an understandable temptation to say: 'The examination groups don't insist on assignment profiling now, so why make life more difficult than it already is?' Of course, that is fair comment, but it happily ignores the discoveries made by recent research into active tutorial work, which indicates that 'students' performance is enhanced by their power to choose and work upon lines of inquiry of their own.' Their being able to do this has to stem from guidance by teachers. We would be foolish to pass up the benefits to be reaped from such dialogue, considering that a sizeable proportion of the job of compiling a profile will be done by students anyway!

6 Departmental Implications

The implications for GCSE as far as department and individual teacher are concerned are considerable, particularly in the early years of the new courses. The more control over assessment that teachers have, the more accountable they are; it's hard not to believe that the examination groups are getting our services cheap, considering the responsibility, the weight of administration and the marking. National noise over increased payment for the assessment work that we undertake would perhaps inspire enough pangs of conscience among the boards to make fairer recompense!

Individually, we shall be obliged to improve upon both teaching strategies and record-keeping to account for the new emphases upon coursework and differentiation. Those of us with experience of coursework already will have devised methods of absorbing the additional administration and of balancing learning and assessment: much more student participation, a longer forward view, pre-tested and readily available resources, and close liaison with colleagues. Departmentally, organic organisation, which gives to all staff a democratic portion of the range of responsibilities, will be the only satisfactory way of assuring the mutually collaborative tactics that can identify potential problems, reduce workloads and generate positive and innovative practice.

ALLOCATION OF RESPONSIBILITY

For departments composed entirely of specialist teachers, this division of labour is an obvious step towards true cooperation and well-oiled efficiency; however, the presence of non-specialist staff, part-timers and temporary teachers will create problems in ensuring that examination requirements are met. Falling rolls mean overstaffed schools; overstaffed schools mean weakened curriculum protection; the headaches for specialists will in all probability derive less from the much-discussed burdens of dealing with oral work and course assessment than from the rapid in-service training of geography colleague F and supply teacher G following the preferment of specialist C. Heads of department will inevitably find their personal resources stretched by the necessity of monitoring the progress made by teachers who are drafted in to plug such gaps. It is therefore logical to encourage the specialists to involve themselves as far as they can manage in the main curricular divisions of the whole work of the department.

Nowhere is this more vital than in the creation and on-going administration of Mode 3 courses; requiring their own external procedures, participation in yet more consortium arrangements, and even assistant moderator duties for other centres, these really are a labour of love. Centres intending to embark upon a Mode 3 will need to appoint a member of department who can oversee the compilation of examination papers, attend to syllabus revision, hold meetings for participating teachers in the department and deal with the mountainous paperwork; it will be obvious that, in such cases, scale points and contractual agreements are the only sensible way of maintaining consistency of organisation.

For the less arduous roles, goodwill must be relied upon; the election of particular people to particular jobs will be an immediate concern in which heads of department will have to exercise the greatest degree of tact and sensitivity. Getting the right match of person and post is crucial; although subsequent rotation of these major roles could be an attainable ideal, the personalities and skills of individuals suggest the desirability of their maintaining control for a number of years of their personal responsibility. The complexities indicate that expertise will be only gradually acquired by experience.

COURSEWORK ASSESSMENT

Once the department has reconsidered its deployment of staff, colleagues will be concerned to establish ways of handling coursework assessment. We shall be responsible to the boards for the effective standardisation of speech and writing throughout the course. Whatever system is decided upon, the inevitable final grading of coursework folders looms ferociously on the horizon somewhere around Easter. However cooperative our inter-staff arrangements have been, the final checking of files and the compilation of grade lists is an extremely time-consuming and painstaking exercise. As our candidates' final grades depend on our consistency and accuracy, we must do the job thoroughly.

Various tactics are possible. Setting a precedent for the release from timetable of all participating staff for at least one day for each course is a must (since other subjects will also be assessing through coursework, this will present school management with a thorny problem!). The numbers of folders in large centres will demand an adequate preliminary grading, so that the main work of the full day consists of the careful scrutiny of grade boundaries. Preparation for this final standardisation meeting has its roots in the cross-checking/cross-marking that teachers need to do early in the course, when a sense of standards is often hazy. At first only individual compositions might be necessary to get the levels right. Later, the value of exchanging the work of whole classes will become apparent, not only in improving the objectivity of staff marking, but also in showing to candidates that the checking is rigorous and reasonably foolproof; certainly in cases where students feel dissatisfied about the marks being awarded by a teacher, second and third opinions can provide reassurance and ease potential friction.

A realistic deadline for the completion of all folios by students and their submission to class teachers must be agreed by the department very early in the course. Bearing in mind the difficulties thrown up by routine checks on the content of files following students' final submissions, together with the chasing-up of backsliders and absentees, we still have to allow students as much time as we can; the deadline will be a reconciliation of these considerations.

Once the whole entry has been assembled, it can be divided either at random with a simple division of the total, or, more helpfully, in batches according to the grades suggested by each class teacher. The sharp focus by one person upon a particular section of the grading system is certainly more reliable, especially when GCSE grade criteria need to be clearly held in

▲ *Fig. 1 'Right . . . now we've checked that everybody's done twelve pieces, that the kids have put titles, dates and their names on, that proper differentiation has been applied, that no malpractice has occurred, that all the assessment objectives have been met and that everybody's done the right balance of closed and open writing, we've just half an hour to grade them before the caretaker locks up.'*

mind. This democratic sharing of the load allows staff to take their section away for perusal at their leisure. Differences of opinion can then be channelled by passing on folders to colleagues dealing with an adjacent grade area. Thus, by the full day standardising session, the spadework will hopefully be complete, and the more refined adjustments can be made.

Corporate Responsibility

The impact of compulsory coursework on departments can be nothing but favourable, since the most disparate of teachers are obliged to work together, to share ideas, and to plan jointly for the future. If we bear in mind that many departments have long since embraced coursework *voluntarily*, there must be a great deal to say for it! The corporate responsibility of the department in dealing with the internal arrangements of assessed courses has a vitalising influence upon the practices adopted in teaching and marking; even at the humblest level, getting together to appraise speech and writing is exactly what we should be doing anyway. The mere fact of enjoying the howlers together does a lot for improving staff relationships and relieving the strain!

Delegation of Work

Though the administrative aspects of the new courses will have the most obvious effect upon departmental organisation, we must not lose sight of the fact that we are primarily concerned with language development, not examination assessment. Good delegation of responsibilities ought to mean that the coordinators of specific courses are actively engaged in regular consultation meetings with relevant staff only, leaving main departmental meetings less clogged with examination administration and better able to deal with methodology, which must not be brushed aside because we have too much to think about in managing the GCSE. Indeed, our successful management of GCSE courses will be dependent on the department's acceptance of a firm foundation of theory and its ability to translate that into practice.

A LANGUAGE FOR LIFE

When an agreed number of coursework assignments has defined what proportion of lesson time remains for other things, we would do well to reflect upon what those 'other things' should be: how do colleagues deal with variety in written styles and purposes, with vocabulary extension, with the basic technical skills of language, with comprehension? What priorities exist for the different levels of ability? These are issues which matter; coursework for final assessment has to be composed against a supportive background of student experimentation with what can be achieved, or progress will be minimal. Coursebooks have always had their limitations, but when such excellent texts as John Seely's Oxford English series and the Oxford *Choices* book are available, it seems sensible to avail ourselves of what they offer: wealth of stimulating material designed to give students experience in using language in many ways, as well as simple explanations of key mechanical points. Once they understand what techniques are available to them, and are committed, they will then handle at their own level whatever we ask of them; our task is to work on the techniques through as many different contexts as we can. The *General Criteria* reference to 'fitness for purpose' is concerned with exactly this. An earlier suggestion that students might go into primary schools could be applied to good effect with the above example: if students know that they will be reading their own descriptive or narrative pieces to a wider audience (and an astute and hyper-critical one at that), they are likely to make a much better job of it than if requested to write for a shadowy moderator/examiner who does not have the incentive power that he or she used to! All in all, then, we need to keep alive the idea of a 'language for life' rather than a language for exams.

RESOURCES

Another departmental consideration will be resources. Relatively small amounts of government money will come our way in the immediate future, hopelessly inadequate for those schools whose annual capitation barely makes ends meet and which are therefore seriously disadvantaged to start with.

Books

Some savings can be made by centres which have previously operated literature examinations with annual expenditure on set texts. Having sets of such literature lying idle on the stockroom shelves for long periods of time is wasteful; the purchase of books purely for examination purposes will at least give way now to the acquisition of stock that will have far more regular use for both language and literature courses at all levels.

GCSE, however, with its recommendations for wider reading, does seem to require more than class sets of readers. Certainly, class sets are not obsolete – the security of learning together through the reading of an entire book is still vital to weaker students, and the experience can be pleasurable to the most able. Teachers and their classes should have common literary ground for discussion and evaluation, since there are so many interesting aspects that students might not otherwise appreciate. Just as a teacher's failure to take deliberate steps towards students' acquisition of new vocabulary and a range of registers in speech can lead to their future linguistic impoverishment, so the glib assumption that private reading will be completely self-sufficient without class discussion will be severely detrimental to their overall development in English.

Class libraries

Nevertheless, the bottom line of departmental spending on GCSE ought to be the provision of readily available resources for students' personal learning programmes. The class library or reading box is a basic essential for all levels; being on hand and full of good reading matter (because its contents are carefully chosen by us), it serves many useful purposes: for a regular silent reading lesson; for individuals' use when other work is completed; for accommodating the broadest range of abilities and for offering students proper choice over what they read. They have disadvantages, too: unless they are reasonably extensive, students can feel that there are insufficient titles to cater for their interests; since the contents must represent a broad spectrum, this can be a valid criticism. Teachers may have to work hard at establishing systematic procedures for borrowing and retrieving books, and also at acclimatising weaker students to the need for getting properly into their reading (many at first wish to exchange their books without really giving themselves a chance).

The problems are not insurmountable, however, and certainly do not counterbalance the gains that class libraries can make. Rotation of individual books and/or the whole boxes may be one way of offering adequate variety, while reluctant readers respond quickly if the books are at the right level. School librarians are often prepared to arrange block loans to classes to make access to books more immediate, whilst at the same time applying their own expertise and informed judgements in the selection.

Purchasing class library books should ideally be done by the whole department, so that the books can be more carefully considered and read before they are bought. There is no shortage of good readers these days, with appealing jackets and contemporary interest; thankfully, publishers have responded well to demands for books for the least able, with simpler language but content appropriate to teenagers. As the GCSE also expects reading of non-literary material, class libraries will benefit from the inclusion of books about hobbies, sport, travel and others of general interest. Magazines may now come into their own; not only do they present factual information with instantaneous appeal, but they also contain very well written articles which employ complex language and vocabulary, which enthusiasts appear to be able to handle without much difficulty. Since classes will provide plenty of reading fodder of this kind, there need be no concern about finance!

Limited GCSE funding will not of course buy complete class libraries at once; the department must agree to allocate over several years a sizeable proportion of annual capitation to this resource; certainly this will not prove universally popular, since many teachers still feel that they wish to have control over the reading done by their classes and will advocate majority spending on class sets. Hopefully, however, the increased pressure of those who recognise that the way to get students to read is to provide huge variety with bags of appeal will carry their point. The GCSE means freedom of choice, albeit along structured lines, and we must acknowledge once and for all that it is simply not necessary to monitor everything that a student reads. If we do, we risk losing the commitment to reading of many young people.

Short sets of books

Apart from class libraries, we should also conserve our money by buying short sets, which have particular value for small-group work and are easily rotated around both class and department. They can be chosen deliberately to give support to assignments both in language and literature.

Equipment

The mad rush for hardware will have already begun, though how much departments can actually acquire will vary from school to school and authority to authority. A cautionary note may be appropriate here. Large numbers of tape recorders, for example, would appear to be crucial to oral assessment, but their use for this purpose is limited. We have already glanced at the logistical nightmare of assessing by cassettes, which in any case cut out important paralinguistic elements of talk.

The choice of audio-visual hardware should be very carefully discussed at a departmental meeting, since every colleague will have different priorities. One might argue strongly for a departmental word-processor, the value of which would become fully apparent if it were installed for staff and student use. Another might contend that a video-camera would also find itself in permanent use, though additional finance would have to be found to buy it in the first place. Overhead projectors and good-quality tape recorders with in-built microphones are splendid for generating oral work, as well as doing service more conventionally as teaching aids. In the end the chief criterion may be 'Which will help the most students?', though life-expectancy is important too.

Television

Television still has the greatest potential for reaching and interesting a majority of students. There is no question that the programmes now available for recording are more than just a handy extra. Whether they are dramatised versions of set texts or, like the *Scene* programmes, are stimulus for thematic work, they should be an integral part of English methodology. A set of *Buddy* and a video tape of the excellent BBC production of this book promises to be one of the cheapest and most widely used resources available to us in the coming year or two. Certainly, therefore, the acquisition of video tapes, blank and pre-recorded, should be high on the list of priorities for GCSE spending.

Filing Systems

Departments will also be aware of the increasing value of good retrieval systems for non-text resources to back up assignments and to reduce the workload in succeeding years. A central bank of single copies with references to their location is the straightforward answer to the exploitation of the many splendid worksheets produced by English teachers. In addition, the colleague responsible for a particular syllabus can build gradually a store of resources relevant to that course, renewing annually depleted stock and adding new material.

Summary

The work of English departments in the coming years will not be easier because of the advent of the GCSE. This chapter alone has indicated the breadth of possible reappraisal (it certainly lays no claim to being comprehensive in its identification of likely issues) that English staff will have to undertake if they wish to refine out of the mass of innovation the nuggets of good practice that will make the whole thing not only workable but rewarding. The perpetuation of single-subject-based curricula must automatically limit the amount of change that we can expect; in fact, English is at the van of progress in GCSE terms, because teachers have for many years been fighting for acceptance of methods that really do work, refusing to allow antiquated examination procedures to dictate the rules. There are those who are very unhappy about change; at Phase Two of the GCSE training, one head of English saw forthcoming retirement as a welcome release from the ever-accelerating revolution in English teaching. We can sympathise, but anyone who doubts that the developments of the past twenty years have been anything but beneficial must have a very blinkered judgement. We can expect similar improvements through further change and must welcome them, even if they do cause temporary discomfort.

Perhaps the crucial point to remember is that teachers of English themselves are the prime movers in inaugurating new approaches to the subject; we have the power to influence change and must therefore exert it. GCSE English has bowed to relentless pressure from forward-thinking practitioners of the subject who want coursework, who want integration of language skills, who reject reactionary kinds of assessment such as the sacred cow of comprehension-passage-plus-questions, who have long been minutely aware of the need for clarity of expression used to present work to young people, and who know what could be done still further to take language teaching/learning into the 1990s. Perhaps now we will begin to find ways of introducing more experiential learning into our own curriculum, of bridging wider curricular boundaries and of banishing the pedagogue altogether! Whatever happens, the greatest aim of all in our work with young people is that they and we should enjoy it.

Appendix
NEA GCSE English Syllabus A, Specimen Examination Paper

This question is referred to on p. 13 in Chapter 1.

Read the story and then answer the questions which follow.

JANE IS A GIRL

He hastily gulped the tea remaining in his cup, grabbed the piece of bread and jam from his plate, started to stuff it into his mouth as he rose from the chair and was stopped by his mother's voice: "Sit down! Where are you going?" and as he went to answer: "Don't talk with your mouth full!"

Jude thought she was most unreasonable.

"Now?" she queried, when she saw he had swallowed the bite.

"Out," he said.

"Mother," she said automatically.

"Mother," he said.

"Be in here at eight o'clock," she said. "Not a minute after. Don't have me chasing you or you'll feel the weight of my hand."

"All right," he said, moving.

"Mother," she said.

"Mother," he said.

"Will I ever put manners into you?" she asked the ceiling.

He was going the back way into the yard from the kitchen, when he stopped and thought. Then he turned and ran up the stairs. He went into a room there. His big brother was in front of the mirror brushing his hair.

"Give us a tanner, Joe," he suggested.

"Get out of here," said Joe. "I want all my tanners."

"Spending them on old girls," said Jude.

He banged the door and ran. Joe didn't chase him. At the foot of the stairs he went into the other bedroom. His sister screamed. She was only half-dressed.

"How dare you come into a lady's room without knocking?" she shouted, hurriedly covering herself.

What a stupid fuss about nothing, Jude thought. "Give us a tanner, Nora?" he asked.

"What do you want sixpence for?" she asked. "Don't use slang."

"Sweets," he said.

"I can only give you tuppence," she said. "It's all I can afford." She reached for her handbag.

"Oh, all right," he said, holding out his hand.

"Go and wash that dirty hand," she said, putting the pennies into it.

"All right," he said. "You smell nice." He said this just to please her. He didn't like all the scents, but that wasn't too bad.

"Close the door after you," Nora said.

He did so, and went to the sink in the yard and washed his hands with the big bar of white soap. He didn't want to go back into the kitchen for the towel so he just went out the back way shaking his hands to dry them.

He went around the corner into the small market-place. There was a shop there. Jude looked into the window. He decided on bull's-eyes which were eight a penny. Each one, uncrunched, lasted for five to ten minutes. That meant nearly two hours of minty sweetness if you gave away only four at the most.

Jude took one from the bag and put it under his tongue. This was the best way to make it last. He went back to his street. It seemed empty, houses on one side facing houses on the other side, their front doors opening on to the pavements. The people were hidden by lace curtains and geraniums in pots. It was a Sunday evening in March.
Jude hoisted himself on the wide window-sill of one of the houses. He knew this was a house where they didn't mind you sitting on the window-sill. Others did. They would roar at you, frightening the life out of you if you weren't anticipating it.

He now shifted the sweet from under his tongue to his cheek and made it bulge there. He knew this would attract custom because, although there didn't seem to be a living soul inhabiting those houses, there would be small eyes watching the street.
Sure enough four playmates to use his sweets on. There were several games they could play. Marbles were not in season, so it would have to be rounders at the four corners where one street bisected the other. On the whole he decided they would play hurling. It was more exciting and would warm him up on a cold evening, so when Jane came out of the house, he took the bag of sweets out of his pocket and looked into it. That brought her. "Have a sweet," he said, handing her one. She took it, so he knew she was enrolled. Pat Fane, Jonjo and Tip Heaney were the other three, so they leaned against the wall, sucking carefully at their sweets. Some of the smaller children also arrived and sat on the kerb or stood with their hands behind their backs, looking, and their mouths watering. Jude knew this was slightly cruel, but how could he dish out sweets to all of them?

He got off the window-sill, crunched his sweet to bits and said: "We will play hurling." They considered this for a moment, and then they ran. He ran himself down the street, around the backs of the houses, into his own yard where he picked up the hurley stick and soft rubber ball. When he got back to the street, the others were scurrying about. His own hurling stick was in good shape. The boss had been broken but he had repaired it with a band of tin that came wrapped around fruit boxes. Jane had a good hurley stick, too, better than his own. The others had makeshift hurleys, that were mostly bits of stick with a crude curve at the end, but they were well used and as precious to them as if they were due to play in an all-Ireland hurling final.

He picked his team. He took Tip Heaney who was the biggest of them and a bit rough, while Jane had Pat Fane and Jonjo. They divided the small ones up between them. The boys took off their coats and put them on the ground to act as goalposts. They sent two of the smallest to each end to watch out for the police, because at this time some of the people took to talking in the Council about the way you couldn't walk the streets of the city without being belted with balls or knocked down with racing kids. Hadn't they homes to go to or the wide spaces of the municipal playing fields? All that stuff, so you had to post sentries.
Jane and himself put the ball in the middle of the street. Then they hit their hurleys on the ground, clashed them three times and then scrambled for the ball. The game was on. It was vigorous. It was interrupted once or twice when irate mothers ran out to take their children's best Sunday clothes from the dusty road, brushing them angrily, and shaking their fists before departing. They replaced the lost goalposts with rocks. Once the ball hit a window and all of them stood like statues waiting for the result, ready to run if the reaction was hostile. Nothing happened so they continued to play.

Jude's side was being defeated. The combination of Jane, Pat Fane and Jonjo was too powerful. Jude himself was fast and slick, but Tip was too slow and heavy, and even the little tricks he used like putting the hurley between his opponent's legs to trip him were unavailing in the end.

So they had to take to argument. It was a goal! It wasn't a goal! It went outside the stone. Didn't it? Yes it did! No it didn't! You stupid idiot, are you blind? The veins in their necks stood out as they tried to outshout one another.

This led to a lot of heat and a lot of vigour. It developed into a furious struggle between Jude and Jane. Each time the ball came to them, they slashed and heaved and threw their bodies at one another until one got the victory and belted the ball away. Sometimes Jane won those struggles and sometimes Jude, and they glared at one another like animals. Now! See! I told you! Jude had cuts on his knees and Jane's stockings were torn. They were egged on by the others. The street was a canon of shrill screams and shouts being deflected into the sky.

This last time the ball was in the air, and they were pressing together looking up, watching its descent. They raised their hurleys to catch it. It came down between them, the ball escaped and Jude fell on top of her.

Now as he fell, shouting, his forehead was practically touching hers. He could see her wide eyes and the bead of sweat between her eye-brows and her white teeth snarling at him from drawn-back red lips. Something happened between them. He saw her face changing as she looked up at him, the excitement dying out of her eyes. He was conscious of feeling different inside himself. This game he had engineered no longer mattered. He was suddenly very conscious that the shape of her body was different from his own.

This is when it came into his mind: Why, Jane is a girl! Jane is a girl! He was suddenly embarrassed. His face was red from exertion before. Now it seemed to him to get redder. He got to his feet. She got up too. She avoided his eyes.

Jude couldn't stand this any longer. He turned and walked away from the field. They were stunned. They called after him: "Hey, Jude! Where are you going? Hey, Jude!"

He was in an agony of embarrassment. He was upset. He wanted to run, but this would look bad. Instead he took the bag of sweets from his pocket, looked at it and threw it towards them. The bag burst and the sweets flew all over the place. They stopped calling then and scrambled for the sweets, laughing. Jane didn't. She had gone to the path and stood there with her back turned. Did she feel the same? he wondered. Did she say, why Jude is a boy?

He went in the back way to his house. He put his hands under the tap. He filled his palms and sloshed the cold water on his face. His face was hot. He washed the blood from his knee cuts so that his mother wouldn't be fighting about them. Then he went into the kitchen. There was nobody there. He sat on the wooden stool in front of the fire, rested his elbows on his knees, his chin on his hands, and he thought. Why should it be different? he wondered. What difference does it make? Now he could see that she had long hair, that she wore dresses, that she was good-looking, but she was a Girl. Wasn't she always one? What was the difference now? Now that he came to think of it Pat Fane was also a girl, and she had fair hair.

"Are you sick or something, Jude?" his mother asked. "Sitting there gazing into the fire. Why aren't you out playing?" He thought he might tell her. But then he didn't. She was always very busy. She sat sewing and listening to the radio. There was a knock at the front door and she put down the sewing and went to answer it.

His sister came down to the kitchen now, ready to go out. She was all dolled up. She looked at the silent boy.

"What's wrong, Jude?" she asked.

"Jane is a girl," said Jude thinking she would understand.

"Say that again," she said.

"Jane is a girl," he said.

"Well, what did you think she was, a rhinoceros?" she asked.

"Hey, Joe, Joe!" she was calling. "Come here while I tell you!"

"No, no!" pleaded Jude.

Joe came downstairs fixing his tie. Nora was laughing.

"Guess what?" she asked. "Jude has discovered that Jane is a girl."

"What, at his age? Not even twelve," said Joe.

Then she was calling her mother.

"Mother, come here while we tell you what Jude said."

Jude fled, his face flaming, towards a green field, as if he was being pursued. He threw himself on the grass. Nobody could find him. He turned on his back and looked at the sky. It was darkening already. There were colours around its edges.

They don't understand, he raged, gripping the grass with his fingers. How could you make them understand and not to be laughing? He remembered going into his sister's room for the pennies. She had covered herself up. She was a girl too, see. Before it had made no difference. Now things were changed. They would never be the same. Never again.

SECTION A. You are advised to spend approximately one and a quarter hours on this section.

1 Look at lines 1-37. Describe Jude's home and family. *(4)*

2 Look at lines 24-62.

For what reasons is Jude so keen to get money? *(3)*

3 Look at lines 38-83. Describe the kind of neighbourhood where Jude lives. *(3)*

4 Look carefully at the way the writer describes the game of hurling from its start (line 78) to the time when both Jane and Jude miss the ball (lines 99-100). By commenting on words and phrases used, show how the writer convinces you that the game meant a lot to the children, and particularly to Jane and Jude. *(5)*

5 What effect does the discovery that Jane is a girl have on Jude's behaviour, thoughts and feelings? *(5)*

6 Study carefully the relationship between Jude and his mother throughout the story. Then write what you think of her as a mother, supporting your views with evidence from the story. *(5)*

7 Sometimes in a story there are passages which have much more meaning after you have read them two or three times, pondering over them. In what way has the passage below hidden meanings which would not appear at a quick reading?
"Instead he took the bag of sweets from his pocket, looked at it and then threw it towards them. The bag burst and the sweets flew all over the place. They stopped calling and scrambled for the sweets, laughing. Jane didn't. She had gone to the path and stood there with her back turned." (lines 113-116). *(5)*

(Total 30)